FLORIDA'S NATIONAL HISTORIC LANDMARKS

Presented by
Bea Hartman

FLORIDA'S NATIONAL HISTORIC LANDMARKS

Copyright @ VAu 1- 049-609

ISBN: 978-0-9998993-4-2

Printed in United States of America on acid-free paper.

All rights reserved. No portion of this book may be reproduced, stored in a retrieval system, or transmitted in any form or by any means, mechanical, electronic, photocopying, recording, or, otherwise, without written permission from the author, Bea Hartman and Florida Preservation, LLC.

Individual permission given for photo utilized. Other photos are credited to the Park Service. All remaining photos are the author's. Inquiries should be addressed to: Hartman0540@gmail.com

ACKNOWLEDGEMENTS

This Historic Preservation book is dedicated to Dr. William Murtagh, a giant in the discipline. His legacy as a leader in Historic Preservation spanned fifty years plus. In 1967, Murtagh became the first Keeper of the National Register, National Park Service, and United States Department of Interior in Washington D.C. During his tenure, he was responsible for establishing and developing standards and guidelines for historic structures, creating a national network for identification and survey that assisted rehabilitation and restoration projects across our country. Bill played a pivotal role in the establishment of Historic Preservation Programs at University of Hawaii (1986), University of Maryland (1984), and University of Florida (1995). Upon retiring in Florida, his current book was published, *Keeping Time: The History and Theory of Preservation* and the book was recently reprinted in Chinese. Bill Murtagh died peacefully in Sarasota, Florida, October 28, 2018 at the age of 95. Many of us, lost a close personal friend.

Thanks are given to Dr. Barbara Mattick, (now retired) was the Bureau Chief of Historic Preservation in Tallahassee for eight years. Alissa Lotane is the new Bureau Chief. Her associate Vincent (Chip) Birdsong and his support staff is in charge of distribution of the Master Site Files and great appreciation is given to everyone.

The author gives photographic credit to the following entities and individuals: National and State Park Service for aerial photos of historic Florida forts. Photographic contributions and opportunities provided by Dr. Bette Boysen and Katherine dePadua are all greatly appreciated.

The author is indebted and give my heartfelt thanks to my many navigators: Victoria Bolduc, Sharon Howgate, Eleanor Lee, and Christine Waterman.

Appreciation is given to Victoria Bolduc, Katherine dePadua, Cheryl Tomas and Diana Waite for providing technical computer information.

Editor Wesley Curry is recognized for his evaluations.

INTRODUCTION

Contrary to what many believe, Florida is not a young state. In 2020 Florida will be 507 years old. St. Augustine is the oldest city in America, forty-two years older than Jamestown, Virginia. With Florida's extensive history, the question is how many National Historic Landmarks does our state support? Florida contains forty six (46) National Landmarks that provides the basis of this book.

"The purpose of the National Historic Landmarks Program is to focus attention on properties of exceptional value to the nation as a whole, rather than to a particular State or locality," National Park Service states. Landmarks are evaluated by the National Park System Advisory Board and designated by the Secretary of the Interior in accordance with the Historic Sites Act of 1935 and the National Historic Preservation Act of 1966. Landmarks are chosen after careful study and meetings by the National Park Service (NPS). Nominated landmarks are identified by theme studies or by special studies that relate to major details of American history. These exclusive documents are reserved in Tallahassee, Florida and Washington, D.C. only. The public can request any document. Great standing is awarded to the Landmark Program.

National Park Service criteria applicable to this text are themes and special reports that are arranged in alphabetical order. Archaeological sites honor Native American life and the Landmark records are displayed in six sites: Crystal River State Park, Miami Circle, Mud Lake Canal, Safety Harbor, Windover and the reconstructed Mission San Luis. Architectural jewels encompass Florida Southern College, Freedom Tower, Mar-a-Lago, Miami Biltmore Hotel and Tampa Bay Hotel. Florida's National Landmarks lists six forts that follow settlement and war issues. The first of these, is Fort Mose and pertains to ran away slaves from the Carolinas. Florida was a secure spot for the slaves. Florida only had one Civil War site, Maple Leaf Ship. The three Seminoles War Sites, Fort San Marcos de Apalachee, Dade Battlefield and Okeechobee Battlefield, present great interest to Historians. These wars were brutal, costly and lengthy. Fort Zachary Taylor assisted the United States in becoming a World Power during the Spanish-American War. Three significant Historic Districts (HD): St. Augustine, Pensacola Naval Air Station and Ybor City are sited. Unfortunately, the records only have two Nature sites, Pelican Island established in 1903 by late President Theodore Roosevelt. The other site is Bok Singing Tower in Lake Wales. Landmark Records include a group of famous authors: Marjory Stoneman Douglas, Zora Hurston, Ernest Hemingway, and Marjorie K. Rawlings. Official residences spotlight Henry Flagler's White Hall and the famous Vizcaya. A new unique preservation site adds a movie set, Norman Film Manufacturing Company and Governor Stone's (Schooner) to Florida's Landmark Program. Outstanding individuals, Mary M. Bethune, Marjory S. Douglas, Henry Flagler and Henry Plant enhance the Florida's Landmark Program. The launch capital of the United States and first in the nation, encompasses all the masterpieces of engineering, design, and architecture functions that moved the Apollo Programs forward. You are privileged to view these documents narratives.

Note to Readers: The information contained in this book is accurate to the best of my knowledge at this time, but as with any research, it may change as new findings appear. While the author accepts responsibility for any errors of interpretations, the author is not responsible for errors and omissions in any resource material used in the writing of this book.

TABLE OF CONTENTS
FLORIDA'S NATIONAL HISTORIC LANDMARKS (46)

1974	BETHUNE, MARY McLEOD HOME	1
1993	BOK TOWER GARDENS (HISTORIC BOK SANCTUARY)	4
1975	BRITISH FORT	8
1984	CAPE CANAVERAL AIR FORCE STATION	10
1970	CATHEDRAL OF ST. AUGUSTINE	14
1990	CRYSTAL RIVER SITE	16
1973	DADE BATTLEFIELD	18
2015	DOUGLAS, MARJORY STONEMAN HOUSE	21
1988	EL CENTRO ESPANOL DE TAMPA	26
1985	FERDINAND MAGELLAN-UNITED STATES CAR NO.1	28
2012	FLORIDA SOUTHERN COLLEGE HISTORIC DISTRICT	31
2004	FORT KING SITE	35
1994	FORT MOSE SITE	38
1960	FORT SAN CARLOS DE BARRANCES	41
1966	FORT SAN MARCOS DE APALACHE	43
1964	FORT WALTON MOUND	46
1973	FORT ZACHARY TAYLOR	48
2008	FREEDOM TOWER	50
1970	GONZALEZ-ALVAREZ HOUSE	54
1991	GOVERNOR STONE (SCHOONER)	56
1968	HEMINGWAY, ERNEST, HOUSE	59
2006	HOTEL PONCE DE LEON	61
1991	HURSTON, ZONA NEALE, HOUSE	66
1992	INGHAM (USCGC) MOVED FROM MT.PLEASANT, S.C	69

1970	LLAMBIAS HOUSE	71
1994	MAPLE LEAF	73
1980	MAR-A-LAGO	76
1996	MIAMI-BILTMORE HOTEL and COUNTRY CLUB	79
2009	MIAMI CIRCLE AT BRICKELL POINT SITE	82
2006	MUD LAKE CANAL	87
2016	NORMAN FILM MANUFACTURING COMPANY	89
1961	OKEECHOBEE BATTLEFIELD	93
1963	PELICAN ISLAND NATIONAL WILDLIFE REFUGE	96
1976	PENSACOLA NAVAL AIR STATION HISTORIC DISTRICT	98
1960	PLAZA FERDINAND VII	103
1998	PONCE DE LEON INLET LIGHT STATION	105
2006	RAWLINGS, MARJORIE KINNAN HOUSE AND FARM	108
2014	RESEARCH STUDIO (MAITLAND ART CENTER)	113
1964	SAFETY HARBOR SITE	117
1970	ST. AUGUSTINE TOWN PLAN HISTORIC DISTRICT	119
1960	SAN LUIS DE TALIMALI (SAN LUIS DE APALACHE)	125
1976	TAMPA BAY HOTEL	130
1994	VIZCAYA	133
2000	WHITE HALL (HENRY M. FLAGLER HOUSE)	138
1987	WINDOVER ARCHEOLOGICAL SITE	141
1990	YBOR CITY HISTORIC DISTRICT	143

MARY McLEOD BETHUNE HOME

641 Pearl Street
Daytona Beach
Volusia County
National Landmark 1974

The National Park Service designated her home, now a museum, as a National Landmark on the Bethune-Cookman University Campus, to honor her. She is honored as a civil rights leader, administrator, educator, adviser to presidents, and consultant to the United Nations. The 1920s vernacular frame two-story structure served as her home until her passing in 1955. Mary Bethune called her home, "The Retreat."

Her humble beginnings began in Mayesville, South Carolina, as the fifteenth child of former slaves. She started working in the cotton fields when she was five years old. Mary accompanied her mother to deliver "white people's" wash. Mary saw all the toys and books. She opened a book, but a white child took the book away from her, saying she didn't know how to read. This critical moment identified her difference, so she walked five miles each day to attend a

Presbyterian Trinity Mission School. Her teacher, Emma J. Wilson, mentored her and helped McLeod attend her same school, Barber-Scotia College, on scholarship, 1888-1893. The following year, McLeod attended Moody Bible Institute in Chicago, hoping to become a missionary in Africa but Black missionaries were not needed. Mary's prime goal was to teach African-Americans, so the family, Mary and her new husband, Albertus Bethune, moved to Palatka, Florida to run a Presbyterian Mission School. She crossed paths with Lucy C. Laney who emphasized character and practical education for girls in the expectation "women will improve the conditions of black people." M. McLeod moved to Daytona for the economic opportunity; "it had become a popular tourist destination and businesses were thriving." In October 1904, Bethune rented a small house for

$11.00 per month and acquired other items from charity. "Bethune used $1.50 to start the Literary and Industrial Training School for Negro Girls. Enrollment was five girls and her son. A year later, she was teaching more than 30 girls at the school.

Booker T. Washington of the Tuskegee Institute advised her of "the importance of gaining support by white benefactors for funding." She "invited influential white men to sit on her board of trustees, gaining participation by James Gamble (Procter & Gamble) and Thomas H. White (White Sewing Machines)." John D. Rockefeller donated $62,000. In 1930's, her friendship with the Roosevelt's, Franklin and Eleanor, added to the network.

In 1931, the Methodist Church assisted with the merger of the Jacksonville boys' Cookman Institute, forming the Bethune-Cookman College, a Junior College. Dr. Bethune became President. In 1941, the college developed a four-year curriculum to achieve full college status and met educational standards of the State of Florida.

Government duties and responsibilities in Washington started to affect her health, so she gave up the college presidency in 1942. She was elected national president of The National Association of Colored Women (NACW) in 1924. Her goals were to hire a professional executive secretary and have the first black-controlled organization with headquarters in the capital. NACW purchased the property at 1318 Vermont Avenue in Washington, DC, as headquarters. Gaining a national reputation, Dr. Bethune worked with five

presidents on Child Health, Welfare, and employment issues. "During World War II, the National Council of Negro Women, (NCNW), gained approval for black women to be commissioned as officers in the Women's Army Corps." National Youth Administration (NYA) created "to promote relief and employment for young people," a program devised by President F. Roosevelt's Works Progress Administration, (WPA). Bethune lobbied so aggressively for minority involvement earning a full-time staff position in 1936 as an assistant. In two years she was appointed Director of Negro Affairs and managed NYA funds. The Civilian Pilot Training Program "graduated some of the first black pilots" in this era. Her close friendship with Eleanor Roosevelt gained her unprecedented access to the White House. She met all the black colleagues working in the federal government. This Black Cabinet met in Bethune's office to discuss issues. The NYA was terminated in 1943.

State Archives of Florida, Bethune working with Eleanor Roosevelt on projects Mary Bethune was placed on journalist Ida Tarbel 1930 list of America's ten greatest women. She received the Spingarn Medal in 1935 from the NAACP. The Dorie Miller

Foundation named her Mother of the Century in 1954. Her Daytona students referred to her as "Mama Bethune." When the United States "Supreme Court ruled in Brown v. Board of Education (1954) that segregation of public schools was unconstitutional, Bethune defended the decision." She passed away on May 18, 1955. Tributes came in from across America-- Atlanta, Oklahoma City, New York, Pittsburgh and Washington-- praising her for her faith in America and the democratic process. Honors and accolades continue. "In 1973, Bethune was inducted into the National Women's Hall of Fame." A monument honoring her was installed in Lincoln Park (Washington, DC), on July 10, 1974. The inscription on the pedestal reads "let her works praise her." The US Postal Service issued a stamp in Bethune's honor in 1985. "Ebony Magazine listed her as one of "50 Most Important Figures in Black US History," in 1989. In 1999, Ebony included her as one of the "100 Most Fascinating Black Women of the 20th Century." Twenty schools across the United States have been named after her. "In 1994, the National Park Service acquired her last residence, 1318 Vermont Avenue," designating it as "Mary McLeod Bethune Council House National Historic Site." In 2002,"Scholar Molefi K. Asante listed Bethune on his list of the 100 Greatest African Americans."

"In 2004, Bethune-Cookman University celebrated its hundredth anniversary from its founding as a primary school."

The University enrollment is now over 4,100 students and thanks to Mary McLeod Bethune for her leadership.

To tour the Mary McLeod Bethune Museum in Daytona Beach, you need to call for an appointment 386-481-2973.

BOK TOWER GARDENS

Lake Wales, Florida
Polk County

National Landmark 1993

This magnificent 130-acre park offers glorious, breathtaking views, and peaceful feelings to millions in this meandering landscape. The "singing" bell tower is the prime focus of Bok Tower Gardens. The tranquil setting offers hours of a serene vista to all visitors. The count is 23 million visitors have toured the gardens since the opening in 1929. The key time to visit is in March when the bloom cycles of azaleas and camellias overlap.

Bok Tower Gardens is located on Florida's central ridge, the highest point, 295 feet above sea level, called Iron Mountain. Edward W. Bok, editor of the *Ladies Home Journal* and wife, Mary L. Curtis Bok, founder of the *Curtis Institute of Music* in Philadelphia, found the ridge while wintering near Lake Wales Ridge. They planned to create a plant and bird sanctuary on this high ridge. Landscape Architect Frederick L. Olmsted, Jr., designed the meandering garden by installing pipes for irrigation, and soil was added for the planting of "1,000 large live oaks, 10,000 azaleas, 100 sabal palms, 300 magnolias and fruit shrubs," states Wikipedia. Sandhill cranes and wild turkeys roam the grounds, along with hundreds of other bird species.

With all the natural beauty, "something was missing." Edward Bok revised his plans. He recalled, "The glorious sound of carillons (bells) of his native Holland," states the Historic Record. The breathtaking Tower construction commenced in January, 1927. The 205-foot tower rests on the site's highest elevation. Architect Milton B. Medary of Philadelphia designed a Gothic Revival and Art Deco tower. A water moat fifteen-foot-wide was built in old English style, serves as a koi pond, gives an additional old-world flavor around the tower. "The Tower is 51 feet square at the base, changing form at 150 feet high to an octagon (8 sides) with 37 feet sides that include sculptures designed by Lee Lawrie" states the Historic Record. The tower features stylish carved screens and friezes ornamentation around the structure. The

Florida Department of State, Division of Historical Resources

Florida Master Site File

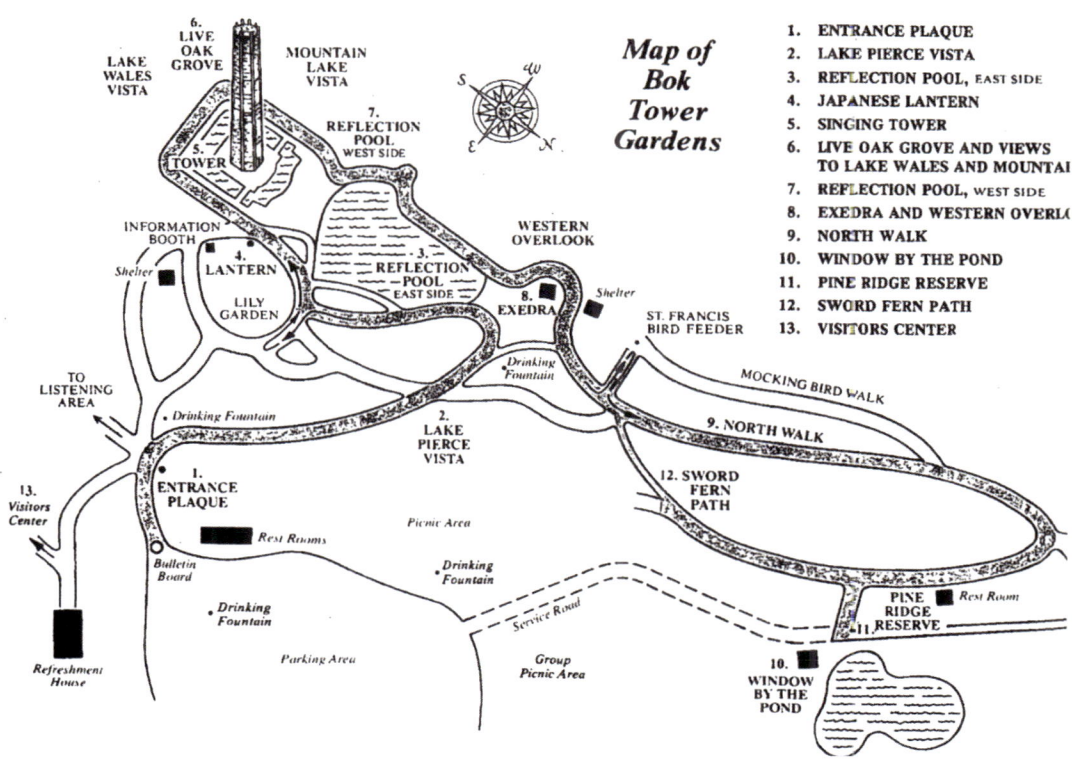

friezes depict Florida's wildlife and, above, this point, the tower becomes octagonal. Tower's building material is "pink Etowah marble and gray Creole marble mined in Tate, Georgia, and coquina stone from St. Augustine, Florida," states the Historic Record.

The only entrance into the Tower is on the north side through a spectacular brass door. The reflective pool mirror images the tower in an alluring manner. Unfortunately, the tower is not open to the public. The tower contains the 53 sweet-tuned bronze bells that occupy the upper third of the structure. The carillon bells were designed by John Taylor Company of Loughborough, England, and installed in 1928. Bok describes the tower as *America's Taj Mahal.*

On the south side is a large sundial, created by Lee Lawrie, but designed by Medary to seal a large opening used to admit the bells.

The Tower's "interior was not designed to be accessed by the general public. Seven functional levels inside contain the Bok Founder's Room (private study), mechanical equipment, two large water tanks, a maintenance and repair shop, the Anton Bees Carillon Library, the carillonneur's office, a practice clavier (keyboard) and the carillon bells" Historic Record states.

President Calvin Coolidge dedicated the Sanctuary (Gardens) and Bok Tower on February 1, 1929, for visitation by the American people in support of Edward Bok. Bok who served as an emblem of success, "rising from an unknown poor immigrant to a wealthy internationally, respected and influential figure. He was always associated with other figures of national significance such as presidents, authors, artists and ministers," Historic Record states. Less than a year later, on January 9, 1930, Edward William Bok died at Lake Wales within sight of the Tower. He had prepared his last resting place at the foot of his beloved Tower, west and slightly north of the Tower's entrance. Bok's crypt is under a simple marker, a nine-foot-tall Japanese memorial lantern, a gift from Usaburo Tsujita of Japan. The gift was interrupted by World War II and did not arrive at the Bok Tower Gardens until July 1955.

Visitors Center built by Mountain Lake Corporation in the 1930s, was acquired by Bok Tower Gardens Foundation in 1983. The Center is now operated by the foundation's staff. The gift shop offers all the Bok's written literature and the Tower Garden construction books and information.

"Since 1928, technical advances made by John Taylor and Company led to the restoration of the bells in 1967," states the Historic Record. The upper twenty-four treble note bells were recast to increase weights." In 1987 four new bells were ordered and installed, providing a total of fifty-seven bells today," Historic Record states. The bells produce almost five octaves in range.

The largest bell weights over eleven tons and the smallest is sixteen pounds. The adjacent site to the tower is 1930's Mediterranean Revival-style mansion Pinewood Estate, built between 1930 and 1932 for Charles Austin Buck, vice-president of Bethlehem Steel Company. Pinewood "was later owned by two other families before The American Foundation" purchase, states the Historic Record. In 1970 Bok Tower Gardens Foundations Incorporated purchased the Pinewood Estate. Bok Tower Gardens utilizes "the house for meetings, lectures, concerts, and guest accommodations. The house and garden are open to the public for tours led by Bok Tower Garden docents" Historic Record states. A majority of Pinewood's original furnishings remain, as it was listed National Register of Historic Places in 1985, known as *El Retiro*, but is not nationally significant. Pinewood is considered "a non-contributing resource for this National Historic Landmark nomination," Historic Record states.

Pinewood's most redeeming quality is the major sight lines of the beauty of the Bok Tower. Edward Bok built the Singing Tower as a gift to the American people for their honorable reception of him, as an influential and powerful leader. Bok was born in Den

Helder, The Netherland, in 1863. His parents moved to the United States when he was six unfortunately his father died soon after the move. At ten, Bok had a part-time job as a stenographer for a New York publishing firm. Bright and enterprising, at 21 years old, events presented to Bok for becoming editor of *The Brooklyn Magazine.* In 1886, he founded a city newspaper service, *Bok Syndicate Press*. Three years later, 1889, Bok became editor of the *Ladies Home Journal,* then he was elected vice-president of the *Curtis Publishing Company,* which published the magazine.

For the next 30 years, "under Bok's guidance, *The Journal* became the most successful publication in mass circulation in the magazine field and a pace setter for the industry," states the Historic Record. Bok and the *Journal* shaped the development of middle-class culture in America, promoting the consciousness of our national needs. "He championed social causes such as teaching hygiene to boys and girls, prenatal education, better sanitation, childcare and public health. He also promoted education and appreciation of music, art and literature; the history of the United States, explaining to women how the government operates and what it is meant to be an American," Historic Record states. The *Journal* was a household necessity.

Another writer called Bok, "a lay preacher to the largest congregation in United States." Bok wrote ten books. His autobiography, *The Americanization of Edward Bok,* won the *Pulitzer Prize* in 1921. He was famous for his philanthropic activities. Bok created, in 1923, the American Peace Award providing $100,000 for the best Peace Plan for the United States to attain with other nations. Bok's Dutch grandmother's precept "You make the world a bit better or more beautiful because you have lived in it." Bok was euphoric with his success in the United States.

Carillon bells perform concerts 365 days a year, at 1:00 and 3:00 p.m. for thirty minutes for the public to enjoy. Should you need additional information regarding Bok Tower Gardens, call 863-676-1408.

Pinewood

THANK YOU

British Fort

Sumatra, Florida

Franklin County

National Landmark 1975

This site has four names attached, British Fort, Negro Fort, Fort Gadsden Historic Memorial and Prospect Bluff Historic Site. The site contains the remains of two forts, British Fort and Fort Gadsden. The chapter holds stimulating historic details for the reader!

British Fort is a symbol of a keen and powerful relationship between runaway slaves and the Seminole Indians. The slaves escaped from Carolinas and Georgia into northern Florida under Spanish control to receive a safe haven with the Seminole Indians. During the War of 1812, the British soldiers, the blacks, and the Indians were mobilized to construct the fort 500 feet from the river bank on Prospect Bluff, near the east bank of the Apalachicola River.

After the 1812 War ended, the British evacuated the area in 1815. However, the British left the fort armed with artillery and munitions in control by 300 blacks and their Indian allies but the fort still flew the British flag. This news alarmed the Americans who referred to this fort as the "Negro Fort".

General Andrew Jackson commanded Colonel Duncan Clinch to attack the Negro Fort in 1816 to protect the American border between Georgia and Florida. From an American gun boat a "hot shot" fired and blew up the fort's powder magazine, destroying the structure and killing 270 defenders. The few 30 survivors were taken prisoner. All these war activities happened in Spanish Florida without Spanish interference. Historic Records state, "Negro Fort is of national significance because its destruction precipitated the outbreak of the First Seminole War, 1817-1818, and the subsequent cession of Florida to the United States in 1821." *History of Florida Forts*, author A. DeQuesada states, President Monroe gave General Jackson, '' the task of solving the Indian problem in the South." These American expansion trends assisted in bringing the entire province under American Rule 1821. General Jackson was impressed with the strategic importance of Prospect Bluff site or the river. Jackson ask, Gadsden to rebuild the fort to protect the supply lines on the river.

Lieutenant Gadsden wrote in his report, "The Defenses of the Floridas" the new fort was a "temporary work, hastily erected, and of perishable materials, without constant repairs it could not last more than four or five years". General Jackson was pleased and named it Fort Gadsden to honor the engineer who had constructed the five star fort. General Jackson maintained a strong garrison at Fort Gadsden to protect against Seminole Indian threat to supply vessels on the river.

In early May, General Jackson "proceeded to capture the Spanish forts in Pensacola and St. Marks". In August President of the United States ordered the forts be returned to the Spanish authorities. "However, Fort Gadsden remained in American hands to protect American interests" on the river. General Jackson was ordered to occupy the St. Marks -- Fort San Marcos de Apache.

The Spanish era in Florida was finally concluded in 1821. Fort Gadsden remained unchanged until the Civil War in 1861. "The river was the breadbasket of the South-its tributaries led into states of Alabama, Florida and Georgia". General Robert E Lee requested "only troops be retained in Florida -- to defend the Apalachicola River--". Fort Gadsden was re-occupied in 1862 but abandoned in July 1863 because of the malaria epidemic. In 1961, "The federal government granted to the Florida Board of Parks jurisdiction over 78 acres for management as a historic site." The grounds contain a smal picnic area pavilion, grills, restrooms, and a display in a kiosk-styles interpretive center.

On the 200th Anniversary, 1816-2016, the National Forest in Florida renamed "Fort Gadsden Historic Site" to "Prospect Bluff Historic Site" at a ceremony on the park grounds. The purpose being multiple sites exist in this one place – a National Historic Landmark. "The National Forest wants the site to have a name that will allow for the full interpretation of its complex history," as stated by Forest Supervisor, Kelly Russell.

Signage for Prospect Bluff Historic Site were placed at the gate. This year, 2018, additional signs will be placed on Highway 65 and Road 129. The park is 6 miles south of Sumatra off of US-98.

CAPE CANAVERAL AIR FORCE STATION

Mission Control Center
Cocoa, Florida
Brevard County

National Landmark 1984

You are welcome to visit the first and foremost Kennedy Space Center/Cape Canaveral in Florida, the launch capital of the United States. The facility is devoted solely to space exploration "since the launch of America's first satellite in 1961." In 1984, the Cape Canaveral Air Force Station and launch pads with their support functions became a National Landmark. National significance encompasses all the masterpieces of engineering, design, and architecture functions that moved the Apollo Programs forward from 1961 to 1975.

The first mission became a reality with America's earth satellite launch on May 5, 1961, with American Astronaut, Alan Shepard. President John F. Kennedy proclaimed, "First, I believe that this nation should commit itself to achieving the goal, before this decade is out, of landing a man on the moon and returning him safely to earth."

The competitive "space race" with the Soviet Union began!

Congress approved development of these marshy, sandy 34- miles long and 10-mile wide strip site on the northern end of Merritt Island. The undeveloped area enabled cape personnel to fuel, inspect, and launch missiles over the waterway without being a danger to nearby citizens; the climate permitted year-round operations. A half-century later, these space achievements bestow on Americans a united pride and honor.

The primary purpose was to have a fixed base from which to launch all space shuttles, including the Skylab and Apollo-Soyuz programs and all future space exploration endeavors.

The Air Force Station consists of discontinuous sites encompassing Launch Pads 5,6,14,19,26,34 and the mobile service tower at Pad 13, and the Mission Control

Room. The blockhouse at launch pad, 5 and 6 is a small National Aeronautics and Space Administration (NASA) Space Museum. Launch complexes 13 and 14 supported the Atlas research and operation programs for a total of 10 Gemini launches from the complex in 1965 and 1966. Launch site 34, constructed in 1959, and supported the Saturn vehicles. Site pad 34 was the launch complex of the flight that took the lives of Astronauts Gus Grissom, Edward White, and Roger Chaffee on January 27, 1967. Launch 26 includes the Air Force Space Museum and is a part of the Kennedy Space Center tour.

The Headquarters Building was built in 1965 and was placed on the National Register in 2000. The NASA Director and his staff occupy a fourth-floor penthouse that is the administration center for the entire program. The building was designed for staff engaged in scientific, engineering, and administrative work.

The four-story building contains 319,000 square feet for the approximately 2,031 persons employed.

Vehicle Assembly Building (VAB) is the largest building in volume at the Space Center; it covers eight acres. The steel-framed structure was designed to withstand hurricane wind loads up to 125 per hour. VAB High and Low Bays and Utility Annex are considered one building. VAB provides four High Bay cells for vertical assembly, checkout, and protective storage of launch vehicles and spacecraft. Two of the four High Bay cells are outfitted for assembly and checkout of Saturn V Launch Vehicles during the Apollo program. The Low Bay is used for shuttle main engine maintenance and holding area for Solid Rocket Booster forward assemblies. VAB is of exceptionally significance because the role of building and designing rockets for the entire Space Program.

Central Instrumentation Facility (CIF) provided instrumentation to receive, monitor, process, display, and record information received from the space vehicle during test, launch, and flight. CIF building was designed in the International style with a skeleton construction of steel and reinforced concrete, marked by rows of ribbon windows. Ribbon windows sit in rows and are the distinctive feature of the style. The International building style describes all the high-rise building at the Kennedy Space Center.

In CIF, special construction features are necessary to properly house electronic and laboratory equipment. CIF is a three-story structure of 136,378 square feet located west of Headquarters building in the NASA Industrial Complex.

Launch Pad 39 built in 1962 and 1968 is labeled AMERICA'S FIRST SPACEPORT. It is the location where man's first voyage from earth to another celestial body began at 9:32 a.m. Eastern Daylight Time, July 16, 1969. The central pad was constructed on an 11-foot thick concrete mat durable base. The site is significant for the Outstanding Civil Engineering Achievements awarded by the American Society of Civil Engineers in 1966. Changing requirements of the space program necessitated the addition of Pad 39-A and 39-B. The new Apollo rockets required more room and stronger facilities than what existed.

Pad A's first launch was Apollo 4 on November 9, 1967. Pad A is significant for the launch of the Apollo 11 mission, July 1969 moon landing with Astronauts Armstrong, Aldrin and Collins, thus accomplishing the Apollo mission. Astronaut Neil Armstrong became a global hero! He stepped on the moon; his famous statement was "one giant leap for mankind."

Launch Complex 39-Pad B (built in 1966/National Register in 2000) was constructed by Bendix-Boeing.

Pad B was specially constructed to with stand the weight, additional heat, and sound, of the Saturn V rockets. Five camera pads cover launches from different positions around Pad B perimeters. Pad B is significant as an engineering and design masterpiece.

Launch Control Center (LCC) retains visual observations of the launch pads from the 450 closed--circuit television consoles, required in each of the four control center rooms. LLC is said to be the "brains" of all prelaunch and launch operations, mission support, and loading controlled at NASA.

The Crawler way was built in 1964/National Register in 2000. An eight-lane freeway, unique highway for transporting the built rockets from the assembly building, (VAB) to the launch pads. The Crawlers, a distinctive mode of transportation, built by Marion (Ohio) Power Shovel Company for use on Apollo and Saturn missions. Maximum Crawler speed is 2 mph when unloaded and 1 mph when loaded. It is

powered by self-contained diesel electric generator units. Each Crawler's length is 131 feet and its width is 114 feet, with a unit weight of 5.5 million pounds. At the time of construction, the Crawlers were believed to be among the largest tracking vehicles in the world. Crawlers were significant for their engineering design.

Operations and Checkout Building (O&C) was built in 1964 /National Registry in 2000.

O&C is the largest (five-story, 601,505 square feet) building in the NASA Industrial Complex. Usage contains crew preparation areas, laboratories, medical facilities, high-altitude chambers, and docking modules in a simulated space environment. O&C is still in active use and is reconfigured to accommodate new needs of the space programs. The training facility is highly significant in space exploration engineering programs.

Press Site-Clock and Flag Pole is reserved for media companies such as ABC, CBS, NBC, CNN, and AP. The careful positioning enables every broadcast to directly frame the public's collective mind worldwide.

The 70-acre Visitor Center site is located six miles east of Titusville on NASA Parkway (State Road 405), and 45 minutes east of Orlando. The Visitor

Center bus tours began July 22, 1966; today, the bus tour is the only way to observe the Kennedy Space Center. For information, you can call (407)452-2121 or visit the web site//www.nasa.gov/office. For educational programs at Kennedy Space Center, call Deputy Chief of Education, 321-867-3623, Lesley.Fletcher@nasa.gov

The REPURPOSE of the Kennedy Space Center, KSC, began when the Space Shuttle Atlantis touched down July 20, 2011. The final landing occurred among cheers and tears. The event produced a loss of 6,036 jobs with the largest lost occurring just two days after Atlantis landed.

NASA'S goal is to "find Commercial partners to occupy the facilities in support of their commercial program and absorb the operations and maintenance (O&M) costs." Maximizing, the benefits of the investments made by the taxpayer, with no additional cost to them. These partnerships have the benefits of bringing high-tech jobs back to the area. NASA's continues to manage a contract for the International Space Station and National Laboratory proceeds.

The Spaceport Planning Office has developed a 20-year Master Plan that will serve for the future of KSC's multi-user partrerships. News reports stated, Boeing Aircraft was one of the new partnerships. The Space Exploration continues and had a prime launching in 2017. The Space Launch System (SLS) is scheduled for 2021 to support flights to the moon and Mars.

CATHEDRAL OF SAINT AUGUSTINE

St. Johns County

National Landmark 1970

April 2013, Viva Florida 500 celebrates the landing of Ponce de Leon in "La Florida," meaning the "feast of flowers." He is believed to be the first European to set foot in Florida. Debate exists on where he actually landed, conceivably South Ponte Vedra Beach, Melbourne Beach or St. Augustine. Ponce de Leon claimed the territory for the Spanish Crown. The King gave Ponce de Leon a promise to govern and colonize the lands he discovered.

A replica of the Ponce de Leon flagship will visit St. Augustine in April 2013 to celebrate the 500th Anniversary of the first European landing in North America. Conquistador Juan Ponce de Leon of noble birth was inspired by a search for riches, gold, and the fountain of youth. Historian Charlton W. Tebeau stated, Ponce de Leon came ashore "probably between St. Augustine and the Saint Johns River" in 1513. Menendez de Aviles founded the oldest continuously occupied settlement in the new world.

On seeing the new land in 1565, Don Pedro Menendez de Aviles, Spanish Admiral from Spain, named the place for his favorite saint, Saint Augustine of Hippo. Days later, he and his followers attended a mass celebrated by Padre Francisco Lopez de Mendoza Grajales in the new land. They witnessed the celebration of religious services across from the present day, La

Plaza de la Constitution that identifies the beginning of Christianity in America.

The Parish of St. Augustine, established in 1594, is the oldest parish in the United States.

Plans for the existing church were prepared by the Royal Engineer Mariano de la Rocque in 1793; construction was supervised by Miguel Iznardy.

Total construction cost was approximately $24,903. The original plan was for a two-story rectangular structure 120 feet long and 42 feet wide. The elevated façade was simple, except for the neoclassic entrance that includes any number of decorative elements. Twin Doric columns on either side of the round arch entrance support the entablature with a classic broken pediment above the door.

When the Diocese of St. Augustine was established in 1870, the church became the Catholic Cathedral of St. Augustine. A fire in 1887 gutted the roof and the interior of the church, leaving only the stone walls standing. New York City architect James Renwick, a long-time winter resident of the ancient city, restored and enlarged the structure. Financial assistance was provided by Standard Oil partner Henry Flagler, who was building his grand hotels designed to turn St. Augustine into the "Winter Newport."

Renwick retained the rectangular shape, but expanded the building 12 feet in the rear, adding large east and west wings, creating a transept, and giving the church a cruciform (cross-shaped) plan. A Spanish Renaissance-styled six-story bell-tower with a tall steeple was added to the west, with a two-story connection to the main building.

Building materials were poured concrete and red clay tile roofing, similar to Flagler's hotels. Renwick placed a statue of St. Augustine, Bishop of Hippo in the old clock niche. Over budget by $20,000, construction cost was $70,000. A wealthy winter resident, John Wilson gifted an eight-day clock with four faces, replacing the burned clock. A sun dial replica like Oxford University's was donated by Rev. Clarence Woodman and was placed above street door on the bell tower.

Archbishop Joseph Hurley in 1965 announced a major church renovation at the celebration of St. Augustine 400th Anniversary. With an extension in the rear, the Cathedral was enlarged by 4,000 square-feet. Wall murals by Hugo Ohlms depicted religious events of historical Florida. The Diocese donated a 204 foot-high cross the "Beacon of Faith" at the Prince of Votive Church on the grounds of the Mission. In December 1976, the status of the church as a minor basilica was raised by Pope Paul VI, honoring the church as a Holy See; only 27 American churches hold this honor.

In recognition of the church's historic significance, a white marble carving of the papal tiara and crossed keys were placed on the arch above the cathedral's main door.

The Cathedral of St. Augustine was designated a National Historic Landmark by the Secretary of Interior on April 15, 1970. A bronze landmark plague was placed on a concrete pedestal on the lawn west of the church in 1972.

When you come to America's Oldest City, visitors are welcome to the Cathedral, 38 Cathedral Place. You can call (904)824-2806 or visit the church's website: www.thefirstparish.org.

CRYSTAL RIVER SITE

CRYSTAL RIVER

CITRUS COUNTY, FLORIDA

NATIONAL LANDMARK 1990

The Archaeological site is the most significant one in Florida and probably the oldest pre-Columbian Indian compound in Florida. "Beginning before the time of Christ, some 2,100 years ago, this beautiful river bank area was a ceremonial center and burial site for about 1,600 years," Historic Record states. Crystal River site significantly advanced and developed "archeological methods and theory" by assisting in the relationship between Florida's coastal tribes and the (southern) Ohio River Valley (Hopewellian) culture. The tribes had direct communication or traveled the rivers. Archeological debate continues over the direct connections of the" Gulf Coast tribes and the Mesoamerican (parts of modern Mexico and Central America or the Yucatan Peninsula)," Record states.

In 1903, C. B. Moore investigation at the site found 450 burials, accompanied with grave goods that indicated trade with Indians hundreds of miles north to the Ohio River. Archaeologist Moore recorded ten temple, burial, shell, and sand mounds. The largest temple pyramidal, mound flat-topped earth and shell mound, placed along the river's edge, is 29 feet in height with base dimensions of 182 by 100 feet. The second flat-topped earth and shell mound placed a short distance northeast from the largest temple mound. The big surprise, the main burial mound, is located halfway between the two temple mounds. Crystal River's circular embankment mounds reflect a Hopewellian practice that is predominantly found at Crystal River site.

Moore unearthed from these a mounds a collections of exotic artifacts, mica sheets, and copper ornaments probably from the Hopewellian culture. Ceremonial stones, two crude stelae (stele) are defined as grave markers. Grave goods obtained through long-distance trade at the Hopewellian " show burials with marine shells, shark, and alligator teeth and other Florida marine products," Record states. Later artifacts found at the Crystal River Site consisted of copper "panpipes", earspools, beads, pendants, and effigy figures, stone gorgets and pendants.

Figure 3-10. Locations of GPR collection grids.

Archeologists present contact between natives of Crystal River and the Yucatan Peninsula. In 1950s, Weisman's debate "centered on exotic artifacts," "complicated stamped" pottery or "negative painted" pottery. He suggests contact with the Mesoamerican, or the Mayan area of the Yucatan Peninsula. Negative painted gourds are similar to the "batik process" and have appeared in Middle Mississippi homeland also.

In 1951 Bullen suggested "three burial types contained in the mounds, prone, flexed and bundle. The record does not identify any purpose for the differing burial types. The Crystal River mounds "span at least 1,600 years of human (native) activity from about 200 B.C to A.D. 1400, and include features built from many cultures," Record states.

On another record page, it stated that Crystal River Site "earliest Indians that settled for any length of time (200B.C - 300A.D.) at Crystal River were those possessing Deptford and possibly Santa Rosa-Swift Creek (Northwest Florida) cultural characteristic. These early settlers started a burial mound built of sand upon an earthen platform," Record states. For the next 1,000 years, " Weeden Island (Old Tampa Bay in Pinellas or late Woolland period) people inhabited the Crystal River site" and build "circular sand embankment up to 6 feet high, " Record states. Mississippian Safety Harbor culture followed, who occupied the site for about a century from 1300-1400. "The larger platform mound also might have been built by the Safety Harbor people, instead of the Woodland Weeden Island people," Record states. This was the mound, Archeologist Moore first excavated in 1903. "This site may contain answers to a number of important questions which have been formed by southeastern archaeologists," Record states.

The 30 acre Crystal River State Park and Archaeological Site, established in 1964, welcomes you to the grounds, open daily

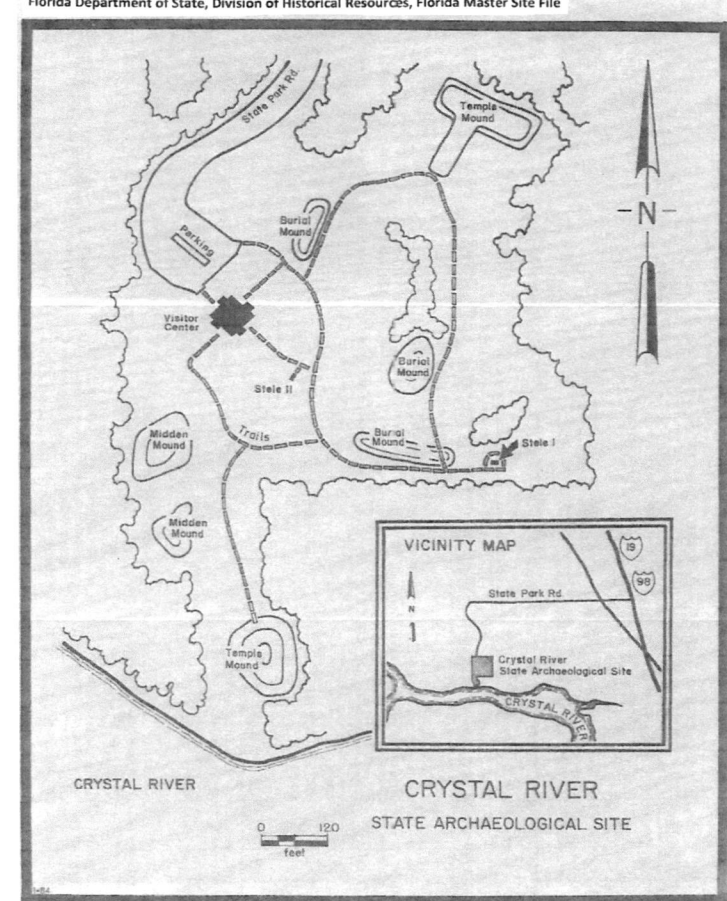

from 8:00 to sundown; call 352-795-3817. The museum is open Thursday through Monday from 9:00 a.m. to sundown.

DADE BATTLEFIELD

STATE ROAD 476
SUMTER COUNTY

NATIONAL LANDMARK 1973

The site is the beginning of the Second Seminole War, December 28, 1835, which lasted until 1842. In the bloody and brutal Seminole massacre of Major Francis Dade's soldiers, 108 died, but 2 survived to tell the gory tale. Chief Osceola opposed President Andrew Jackson's policy of Indian removal to Oklahoma.

The massacre was the worst loss suffered by the U.S. Army. Major Dade from Fort Brooke (near Tampa) who was enroute to Fort King (near Ocala) to reinforce the small garrison at Fort King, 100 miles from the beginning point. Indian eyes watched their every step of the way, from behind the palmetto bushes. A mystery occurred preceding the battle. Major Dade hired a Negro slave named Luis Pacheco as a guide to escort the army over the primitive wooded trail. Major Dade's group included "eight officers and 100 men, four oxen, a six-pounder cannon, and a light wagon carrying provisions for 10 days. The guide would disappear from the party for days, always returning to report that he saw no Indians" the Historic Record states. The massacre occurred two miles south of the present day Bushnell exit on U.S. 301. The

Florida Archives

other survivor was the guide, Luis, who disappeared during the fighting. Luis reappeared in Florida, 40 years later, approximately 1875, but denied he betrayed the troops. Luis pretended to fall at the first shoot and was taken by the Indians after the battle; so he declared!

"General Gaines arrived on the scene, seven weeks later, February 20, 1836, identified the bodies, and gave them a proper burial with military rites. Gaines placed the officers' bodies on the east side of the trail, and the enlisted men in two graves within the redoubt. August 15, 1842, the army officers contributed funds to pay for a second interment of Major Dade's troop at the National Cemetery at St. Augustine," Record states.

The Natives had a deadline to leave Florida, beginning January 1, 1836, under the terms of the Treaties of Payne's Landing (1832) and Fort Gibson (1833). Prior to meetings before 1832 with the Seminoles near St Augustine in 1823, the white men were forcing the Seminoles to settle on a gameless, barren reservation area, between Ocala and Charlotte Harbor, known as the "Hungry Lands" to the Indians. "The reservation was the first of a series of unsuccessful attempts to control the Seminoles by placing them on a reservation. The expanding white population intruded almost immediately into these poor lands, and two races were once again in sharp and bitter conflict," Historic Record states.

Behind the resistance to removal was the brilliant and aggressive Chiefs Osceola, Jumper, Wildcat and Micanopy who resisted the Indian Removal. "Osceola's plan was three fold: (1) terrorize collaborators preparing to accept removal by murdering passive Chief E. Emathla, who was steadfast in his determination to leave Florida; (2) kill Indian Agent Wiley Thompson, who shamed him and his people; (3) destroy the feeble American forces in Florida," Record states. All three events evolved quickly.

The "Second Seminole War was the longest and most costly Indian war ever fought in the country," Record states. During the next eight war years, nearly 1,500 soldiers died of wounds or disease. The war cost to the Federal Government was estimated to be at least 20 million dollars.

Dade Battlefield State Historic Site or Memorial Park consists of 80 acres, marked by a stately arch over the entrance. Monuments mark the space where the gallant officers and soldiers fell. Acres of pine flatwoods and live oaks have turned the spot into a Florida beauty memorial. The museum displays artifacts, 350 brass military buttons, buckles, rifle balls, and teeth. These artifacts are mounded in a glass-fronted case, prepared by Florida State Museum in Gainesville. The Park's contact number is 352-793-4781, and it is open 9:00 a.m. to 5:00, Monday to Friday.

MARJORY STONEMAN DOUGLAS HOUSE

3744-3754 Steward Avenue
Miami, Florida

National Historic Landmark 2015

Floridians were favored to have Marjory Stoneman Douglas reside in Florida for 70 plus years. "Douglas was an accomplished journalist, poet, short story writer, and keen observer of South Florida politics, society and the environment who was at the vanguard of the women's reform movement in Florida," states the State Historic Record. She was one of Florida's first environmentalists who activated the national environmental movement in the 1980's.

Stoneman Douglas other great accomplishments was her insight, understanding, education and awakening of citizens, when she wrote her book: *The Everglades: River of Grass.* She was a distinguished Florida Citizen who saved Miami's water supply.

Marjory Stoneman Douglas was born in Minneapolis, Minnesota, in 1890. Her parents separated when she was six years old, and she was raised by her maternal grandmother in Taunton, Massachusetts. Even at a young age she had an insatiable appetite for reading. Her mother's mental health deteriorated and she died the year Douglas graduated from Wellesley College. She drifted with college friends and had unsuitable jobs. Unknowingly, she married a con artist, Kenneth Douglas. Her uncle encouraged her to move to Miami in the fall

of 1915 and she reunited with her father, Judge Frank Stoneman, who had just established *The Miami Herald.* Stoneman Douglas transferred her "unrelenting passion" to make the world a better place for her and for the citizens of Florida.

The themes of the Stoneman Douglas record are her home (workspace) and the restoration of the Florida Everglades. The bungalow served as her writing laboratory, her workspace, and her lifelong home for more than 70 years. Architect George Hyde designed the Masonry Vernacular Cottage in the 1920s Dade County architecture style. In 1926, Marjory Stoneman Douglas was proud of her home because single women of her day seldom owned their homes. She said, it is the house that *Saturday Evening Post* built, with the income from her short story writing.

The interiors had the sleeping quarters and bathroom with a large living room filled with books and research materials. The kitchen did not have an electric stove but a hot plate for cooking, toaster, ice box to store food. One report stated she had a one window air conditioning unit; another reported no air conditioning. Douglas was happy with the reasonableness and openness of her home. Open to the ocean breezes, flowers, birds, inspired her, as she penned her short stories and books on the back patio. Douglas completed novels and *The Everglades: River of Grass* on her back patio. In her 80's, she founded Friends of the Everglades and ran the organization from her Steward Avenue home.

After turning 100, Douglas held press conferences on her large front yard. In 1991," Florida Governor Lawton Chiles sat in a folding chair in the front yard of the Douglas home and signed a multi-million dollar cleanup of the Everglades," confirmed in the State Historic Record.

Today, the updated Douglas' home is owned by the State of Florida, under the care of Florida Park Service with a park ranger resident maintaining the property. The home's electrical system was updated for safety purposes and central air conditioning was installed; in addition the floors were restored. Historic Resources Department gave their approval. In 2015, her home become a National Historic Landmark under the criterion it is where Florida's first eminent environmentalist lived and died.

Douglas departed from fiction writing from 1930 to 1940s, but her "endless intellectual curiosity served her well"; she turned her attention to a young discipline, "ecology" states the Historic Record. In this time frame, her 1943 book, *Miami River, South and the Everglades,* was published. Douglas continued to study scientific data, compared notes and interacted with many scientist over the function and purpose of the Everglades. In this time frame Douglas interacted with Gerald Parker, a scientist with Miami Water Resources Division office who mapped saltwater intrusion coming into potable water wells. Parker was the first to solve and interpret the "system of aquifers" and how these aquifers are replenished from "rainfall over the Everglades, thus effecting all South Florida's drinking water," states the Historical Record. Parker named the Miami system'' the Biscayne Aquifer" which was filled by the Everglades. Parker proposed a series of "saltwater control dams" to keep freshwater levels high and preventing saltwater intrusion. This was the "first time scientific study dictated a procedure in Everglade's water control, marking the beginning of constant monitoring of the fragile Everglades environment," Historic Record stated.

Marjory Stoneman Douglas consulted with University of Florida Professor John Goggin, an expert on Florida's native people and their circumstances, living in the Everglades. Her conclusion, of the Everglades complex ecosystem systems, and was described as a whole, "Kissimmee-Lake Okeechobee-Everglades watershed", and should not be isolated as just the Everglades, Historic Record stated. Douglas sat on the back patio of her Steward Avenue home, and wrote in longhand, comprehensive assessments of the Florida Everglades. Douglas penned her tour de force, *The Everglades: River of Grass.* Published in 1947, the book enjoyed twenty printing by five separate presses that sold over 10,000 copies annually. Her masterpiece became the definitive interpretation of the Everglades, by redefining the concept of the Everglades as a valuable river instead of a worthless swamp. She defined the Everglades as a "wetland" that shall be valued for restoration. The book's opening sentence is "There are no other Everglades in the world," thus placing the immense importance on the Everglades. Over time the Everglades restoration saved Miami's water supply. In 1947, the Everglades, southwestern portion was dedicated as the Everglades National Park.

Her speaking demeanor and grandmotherly image served her well, giving her an upper hand over the opponents. She was five feet, two inches tall, weighted 100 pounds, appeared to be half the size of others on the podium. Douglas dressed immaculately with pearls, floppy hat, gloves and big sun glasses, speaking with a cool-head, fiery speech, strong and with unrelenting passion. The press loved her, calling her, Our Lady of the Glades, Empress of the Everglades, Guardian, Mother Teresa, and Grande Dame of the Everglades. *St. Petersburg Times* writer Klinenberg said, "She had a tongue like a switchblade and the moral authority to embarrass bureaucrats and politicians that made things happen". She had everyone's attention! "Photographers shoot upward, --- giving her the imposing quality of an aged crusader—long life and undiminished vigor," Historic Record states.

In 1969, Douglas-at the age of 79- launched Friends of the Everglades to fight the proposed "jetport" attempting to be built in Big Cypress portion of the Everglades, a fragile ecosystem. Douglas spoke to all organizations that would listen, receiving 15-20 new members at $1 each. "In a year Friends of the Everglades had 500 new members, another year 1000 members, and year later 3,000 members from 38 states", *Voice of the River,* Rothchild states. This was the beginning of the National Environment Movement and our quality of life positions that have critical consequences.

Dade County Port Authority declared, damaged their image in the media by declaring, "a new city is going to rise up in the middle of Florida--- whether you like it or not," Historic Record stated. National figures spoke out against the Florida "jetport", Wisconsin Senate Gaylord Nelson, and U S Geological officials , "drainage would destroy South Florida ecosystem and the Everglades National Park", Historic Record stated. Shortly, Florida's Governor, Rubin Askew and President's Nixon's Secretary of the Interior agreed, the "jetport project" should be relocated elsewhere and stopped the funding to the jetport's developers. Big Cypress became a National Preserve in 1974. This massive tract of the Everglades plays an important role in recharging the Everglades' hydrology.

In the 1980s, Governor Bob Graham drafted his "Save the Everglades" program with three experts: two were professors and the third Marjory Stoneman Douglas. Graham announced a phased restoration of the Kissimmee River in 1983.

Douglas received a multitude of awards for her continuing efforts for the protection of the Everglades. The Department of Environmental Protection named its new headquarters in Tallahassee in her name in 1980. *Ms. M*agazine honored her as "Women of the Year". In 1991, Stoneman Douglas was honored with a visit from Queen Elizabeth II, she gave the Queen a signed copy of *Everglades: River of Grass*. Two public schools were named in her honor. In Miami-Dade County an Elementary School, a park, and a street are named for her. Broward County named a High School in her honor. In 2018 the Marjory Stoneman Douglas High School on February 14th, Valentine's Day, witnessed a most tragic event: 17 innocent people lost their lives in a shooting. This devastating event disgraces the memory of Stoneman

Douglas's name. She was inducted into Florida Women's Hall of Fame. In 1993, President Clinton awarded her the highest honor given to a civilian, the Presidential Medal of Freedom. Douglas donated her award to her alma mater, Wellesley College.

Blindness did not slow her down. She shifted to talking books and dictated letters to her three assistants. Blind from macular degeneration and with diminished hearing Marjory Stoneman Douglas died at the age of 108 in her home on May 14, 1998. "Her ashes were scattered over the 1,300,000 acres of the Douglas Wilderness Area in Everglades National Park," states Wikipedia. Friends said, "The silence is terrible" but opponents said, death was the only thing that could "shut her up."

Marjory S. Douglas receiving a state award from Governor Graham and his cabinet.

EL CENTRO ESPANOL DE TAMPA

Tampa, Florida

Hillsborough County

National Landmark 1988

The first and oldest club was established in 1891 in Ybor City, known as Tampa's Latin Quarter. The mutual aid social club served and was enjoyed by its membership for 92 years. Adaptive reuse granted transformation of this famous historic landmark to a new use, for all to appreciate.

An anti-social atmosphere existed against the Spanish and, to counteract these conditions. Spanish organized a mutual aid club. "The first clubhouse, at 16th Street and 7th Avenue in Ybor City, was an ornate wooden building that contained a theater, dance hall, cantina and classrooms," Historic Record states. The club Centro Espanol was a success that had generous financial and moral support. Their membership expanded swiftly to 926 in 1901 and to 2,687 in 1908. The small structure was inadequate for the expanded membership. A decision was made to build two new social clubs with the same amenities. One, in Ybor City, El Centro Espanol de Tampa; the other one in West Tampa, at 2306 North Howard Avenue to serve the Spanish community. This structure is in a long term lease with the City of Tampa.

Ybor club architect Francis J. Kennard designed a French Renaissance Revival style building with heavy influences from Moorish Revival and Spanish Mediterranean Revival styles. The two ½ story red brick structure with white stone accents faces 7th Avenue and features an arched main entrance with cast-iron trim. Both structures, Ybor and West Tampa, were completed in 1912.

During World War I, the immigrant membership thrived. The prosperous middle class and the second generation grew up and enjoyed performances by stars of the Spanish-speaking world, and the ballroom was lively. Medical services provided superior care. The Great Depression hit the community hard; since cigars were a luxury item, demand went down. "Cigar workers lost their jobs and stopped paying their club dues. Others moved out of the community to look for different work," states the Historic Record.

During World War II, December 7, 1941, "El Centro Espanol and the other ethnic clubs of Tampa lost much of their vigor". Government changes, social and cultural brought immigration restrictions that "stopped the flow of new, young immigrants from Spain, Italy, and the West Indies, which sustained the clubs" Historic Record states. Federal law of prohibition, forbidding the sale of alcoholic beverages, suppressed the Latin Club life. In this time frame, children of Latin community mixed with the larger population and became "Americanized" and were not interested in joining the social clubs.

In the early 1980's, surrounded by the above issues, El Centro Espanol gave a priority to the maintenance of the clinic, but sold the club building in 1983. The building remained vacant for years. The new owners planned for adaptive reuse; buildings that have outlived their original use, but they lacked funding, land use change or redevelopment knowledge.

 In 1998, new development committed $55 million to the project with upgrades of 200,000 square feet complex, fronting 9th Avenue East and attaching to Centro Espanol by a street walkover. Upgrades to the club included $5 million for air conditioning and structural improvements and a name change to Centro Ybor. Centro Ybor combines two structures in shopping complex/ entertainment center and mix of uses, on 7th Avenue, completed in 2001. Centro Ybor establishment has a 10 movie screen AMC theater, 3 restaurants, 3 retail shops with space for office use.

For meaningful appreciation, take a walking tour to witness the resilience, culture and heritage of the Ybor City Community Development and the redevelopment. Ybor City Ambassadors provide friendly guides and assist visitors, also email your inquiry to YborAmbassador@tampagov.net, to contact Ybor City Development Corporation at (813) 274-7936.

FERDINAND MAGELLAN - UNITED STATES CAR NO.1

12450 Southwest 152 Street
Miami/Dade County
National Landmark 1985

The author wishes to introduce the readers to the "White House on Rails." In 1942, the Pullman Company adapted the private car, "Ferdinand Magellan," for exclusive presidential use. One of America's most famous railroad cars is a National Historic Landmark with a distinctive designation, as a "moveable" landmark "U.S. Car No 1" is historically significant for its association with three Presidents. The secret code words used, "POTUS-PRESIDENT of the UNITED STATES," when the train moved over the rails.

Presidents Franklin D. Roosevelt, Harry S. Truman and Dwight Eisenhower utilized "Ferdinand Magellan" for official use. The 1942 presidential retrofit included armor-plating of 5/8-inch steel to the roof, floor, sides, and ends. These reinforcements raised the weight of the car to 285,000 pounds, twice the normal weight. This necessitated the replacement of the running gears, new roller bearings suitable for heavy-duty construction, and other safety features. Doorways were reconstructed like modified battleship bulkheads. They were water and airtight.

Protective bulletproof glass, three inches thick, was added to all windows. On the roof, submarine type escape hatches were installed. In addition, all furniture and fixtures were bolted in place. President Roosevelt installed elevators on the rear platform; these were removed during the Truman administration. All other features remain today.

The train's exterior is painted the standard dark Pullman green with standard lettering; there was little indication of the presidential status of the train. The rear platform and steps are also green with brass rails, handles and lamps. Loudspeakers were attached to the roof top of the train.

Interior changes from the private Pullman configuration were made to accommodate the Presidents. One stateroom was removed to accommodate a more spacious dining room, allowing seating for 12 plus. The President's suite contained a full-size bed, placed transverse to the car. A build-in wardrobe, dresser, and chair were also included. Shower-bathroom was near the room's rear.

President Roosevelt set a travel record with 399 trips, and 213,827 miles by rail, moving at a leisurely speed of 35 miles per hour. President Truman requested that the speed be increased to a racing 80 miles per hour. This produced a major concern for the train's conducting engineers. In 1948, President Truman used the "Magellan" for his whistle-stop campaign of 21,000 miles which resulted in his election upset of T. Dewey.

Presidential trains had the right-of-way over all other railroad traffic. Opposing trains stood still until the special train and the complete entourage of 15 to 18 cars had passed. No train followed the Presidential trains closer than 15 minutes' running time. Further railroad safety procedure involved a pilot locomotive preceding the Presidential train; bridges were given extra scrutiny; additional track walkers were employed. The World War II backdrop demanded these heavy security strategies.

President Eisenhower used the train only twice, once on an overnight visit and another on a trip to Canada. In January 1954, Mrs. Eisenhower made the last official journey on "U.S. Car No.1," on a trip to Connecticut to christen the first U.S. atomic-powered submarine, Nautilus.

In April 1958, the United States government retired the "Magellan," removed the communication equipment from the train and transferred the car to the University of Miami for placement in the Gold Coast Railroad Museum. In November 1966, the entire railroad museum was relocated from Fort Lauderdale, Florida and due to road construction of I-595 in Broward County. The entire railroad museum moved to southern Dade County at the present location, www.goldcoast-railroad.org or call 305-253-0063.

"Magellan" represents an era when rail travel was the speediest choice of travel.

This unique train is the predecessor to "Air Force One." The first president to travel by train was Andrew Jackson in June 1833. He

traveled only 13 miles from Ellicott Mills, Maryland, to Baltimore to demonstrate the new charter, Baltimore to Ohio (B&O) Railroad line. Abraham Lincoln established the whistle stop technique in 1858, when campaigning for United States Senator. President Warren G. Harding installed loudspeakers on the rear platform for whistle stop tours to address large crowds. In 1911, President William H. Taft is credited with a six weeks' campaign tour, the longest presidential train trip.

  Conference room on the train.

Water Dome

FLORIDA SOUTHERN COLLEGE HISTORIC DISTRICT

111 Lake Hollingsworth Drive, Lakeland

Polk County

NATIONAL LANDMARK 2012

"The Princeton Review dubbed Florida Southern College as "The Most Beautiful Campus in the Nation." This treasure is being resurrected. The campus buildings are the largest single-site collection of architect Frank Lloyd Wright's work in the world. The site is significant as the only college campus Wright designed. Wright was one of America's most influential architects. This campus provides a very rare statement about the architect's work.

In 2007, the buildings were placed on the watch list of 100 Most Endangered Sites worldwide from the World Monuments Fund. The Monuments Fund listing raised needed awareness of the restoration project's funding. The organization endorsement announces that the site collection of buildings is significant for the world to save. Private grants and state funding allow Wright's architectural structures to survive. The preservation projects are ongoing in 2019.

Events unfolded that began a trusting partnership between master Architect Frank L. Wright and the ambitious College President Dr. Ludd M. Spivey, who appeared on Wright's doorstep in Spring Green, Wisconsin, in 1938. Spivey's inspiration was to expand the campus in an ultra-modern style and away from the traditional architectural concepts of the 1930s. Wright was impressed by his boldness. Wright promised to visit the campus; Spivey promised to raise the funds.

Wright liked the site's sandy soil and the 100-acre orange grove campus gently sloping to Lake Hollingsworth. In a year Wright had devised a detailed master plan for the new campus. The two men agreed with a handshake – a gentlemen's agreement, without a written contract or a mention of stipend. They had a meeting of the minds; trust was established.

Wright titled the Florida Southern College campus project "Child of the Sun," which evolved during his "Organic Architectural Period." The idea of organic architecture transfers not only to the buildings' relationship to the natural surroundings but to the buildings' design. Wright believed structures with their natural surrounding by growing naturally and blending with their environment. Modernist architects took the idea of organic architecture to new heights by using new forms of concrete and cantilever trusses, creating swooping arches without visible beams.

Wright's 1939 Master Plan called for 18 buildings. Ultimately, twelve Wright-designed structures were built, including the esplanades (covered walkways) and the water dome.

Originally, college students performed the work in exchange for tuition reduction (sweat equity, as it is called today). The first student-built structure, Annie Pfeiffer Chapel, was built from 1939 to 1941.

Anne Pfeiffer Chapel

The student workers built the wall supports with a mixture of concrete and crushed coquina that was placed in wooden forms and allowed to harden overnight. The next day the blocks were sprayed with water, allowed to cure for several days before being installed. The blocks were held in place with steel-reinforced rods that have rusted over time and are now failing. The 70-year-old structures have been exposed to continuous weather action, moisture, and sun, causing major deterioration.

The block's holes are filled with colored glass and are visible from inside the chapel during the day, but at night the glass hues are visible from the outside. The wall blocks technique was developed by Wright and symbolizes his creativity.

The three-year construction period stretched to 20 years. World War II impacted the building progress. Male students enlisted to serve in the war. Female students built the next structures, E.T. Roux Library and Thad Buckner that was erected in 1945. During the war years building materials and funding were in short supply.

The first building, Emile Watson and Benjamin Fine Administration, constructed by an outside firm with Wright supervising, was concluded, in 1948 as well. The picturesque stunning Water Dome was restored completely in 2008. The Water Dome is activated four time periods daily.

The integrated classroom and seminar buildings, Carter, Wallbridge, Hawkins, Raulerson structures were concluded, in 1943, and now connects into one configuration. The imposing Ordway Building, finalized in 1952, is now used for industrial arts. The appealing William Danforth Chapel, erected in 1955, retains the original pews and cushions designed by Wright.

Built in 1958, the Polk County Science Building holds the only planetarium Wright designed and built at a cost greater than $1 million. This building illustrates Wright's molding of space. His use of low-ceilings, compressed corridors and foyers that opens abruptly into expansive spaces which emphasize the difference in spatial uses. The building's floors are painted Cheyenne Red, Wright's favorite color.

Innovative thinker Wright planned the "Esplanades." 1.5-mile covered walkways connecting all the buildings. The purpose was to protect the students from the sun and Florida's heavy summer rains.

Esplanades Walkway

Wright appeared youthful at 70 years. When his new campus project commenced, he traveled by train from Wisconsin and often slept on the bare concrete floor at night in one of the buildings. His visits to Lakeland aroused a stir during the 20-year building period. Lakeland residents came out to see the handsome white-haired man with his walking cane, his pork-pie hat, and his flowing cape that protected him from the sun. Residents held him in awe and did not ask questions of him.

The world lost Frank L. Wright in 1959. Wright's architecture at Florida Southern College was his virtuoso performance. The college welcomes your visit and financial support for the ongoing restoration projects.

You can call the college, (863) 680-3891, to make a contribution, or visit www.flsoutherm.edu/fllwctr/index.htm.

From Lakeland in Polk County your visit should continue south, to Lake Wales and go to Bok Tower.

FORT KING

3925 East Fort King Street
Ocala, Florida, 34470
Marion County

National Landmark 2004

The proclamation is "We will rebuild the Fort". The ground breaking ceremony occurred May 19, 2017 and attended by many citizens and officials. Land is cleared and expanded to 40.47 site acres from 19.63 acres. The project's generous funding came from a State Matching Grant paid almost half of the $653,000 reconstruction cost. Additional funding came local donations, 210 private individuals, private foundation grants, local private companies donating materials, time, another Grant from City and County funding. Another spectacular program called "Buy a Log and Build a Fort" contributed funds. Fort King Heritage Association (FKHA) is a Florida not-for-profit corporation formed to protect, preserve and develop the history of Fort King. The spectacular new fort will be built on a same hill in the same style, as the original 1827 fort, thus preserving exceptional historic value.

Fort King was the main stage in the advance of the frontier settlement in Florida. Fort King was constructed to administrate the Treaty of Moultrie Document that relocated the Seminoles to central Florida and promoted law and order in the wilderness. The Seminoles trusted the Indian Agency and the Great Father (U.S. President John Quincy Adams). The recession of 1829 brought budget cuts and Seminole were left without soldiers to protect them from bandit white settlers. Fort King stood empty for 3 years (1829-32).

The government reduced the Seminole annuity to a low level so they could not buy enough corn. Seminoles began to starve, but they did

not touch Fort King for the wrongs that occurred.

The terms of the Moultrie Treaty were broken. "May 1832, a new Great Father, President Andrew Jackson, made the Seminole sign a new treaty at Payne's Landing on the Ocklawaha River". The soldiers returned to Fort King. The fort did not become a symbol of freedom and hope. Seminoles were told they must leave Florida forever.

A new challenging warrior appeared on the stage, rejecting the United States orders to leave Florida and threated War, unless the Seminoles were left alone. All trust was gone, but the Indian Agent Wiley Thompson was not provoked by the warrior rising among the Seminole ranks. When the Warrior Osceola became unruly, "Thompson seized him and put him in chains". Seminole vengeance is next course of action and the start of the Second Seminole War.

June 1834, came a new Warrior, OSCEOLA. His father was English and his mother, a Creek. Osceola grew up in a white society, using the name Billy Powell.

In the late afternoon, Osceola waited in the forest for Indian Agent Thompson to appear, walking around the stockade grounds. Osceola and his warriors fired and Thompson fell, riddled with fourteen bullets that marked the beginning of the second Seminole War, December 28, 1835. The same time "reinforcements under Major Francis Dade were marching up from Fort Brooke (Tampa)." Seminoles ambushed the unit. The second Seminole War lasted for seven years, the longest and costly Indian War in United States History.

Osceola forcefully opposed the determination of the United States government to remove their people to a new land, in what is now Oklahoma. Fort King was abandoned in May of 1836 and warriors burned the fort to the ground but the fort was rebuilt in 1837. Somehow, the Seminoles escaped to the Everglades and others relocated to western lands.

Osceola camped at Moultrie Creek where the Treaty was signed 14 years earlier, giving the Seminoles a huge 4,032 acres Reservation in central Florida. Later the Moultrie Creek Treaty was nullified, asking the Seminoles to leave Florida. Osceola wanted to confer with General Thomas Jesup under a Truce Pact. General Jesup dispatched General Joseph Hernandez who found Osceola's camp marked with a white flag. Hernandez and troops surrounded the Seminoles. Osceola surrendered. After capture he was transferred to Fort Moultrie at Charleston, South Carolina. Osceola passed away a year later, January 30, 1838, probably from chronic malaria illness.

The Second Seminole War terminated in August 1842 and the last troops withdrew from Fort King. Newly formed Marion County designated Fort King as the first county seat in 1844. The two-story cupola-topped barrack became Marion County's first courthouse. A new post office, a Methodist mission and general store surrounded the courthouse. The courthouse moved to their new building in September 1846. The fort was salvaged for building materials in Ocala. A one-acre tract in the southwestern portion of Fort King was purchased by the Daughters of the American Revolution to honor those who died during the Second Seminole War. The fort site was purchased by the McCall family and recently City of Ocala and Marion County repurchased the Fort King site and own the property jointly.

New Fort King

First construction phase, the stockade, is now complete, October 22, 2018. Kudos to the fort builders for their rapid work. Fort walls stand sixteen, 16, feet tall with an additional 2 feet anchored in concrete for durability. The termite treated red pine timber logs were imported from upstate

New York. The next project will be the blacksmith shop built on the outside of the fort. Archeology studies estimate a time line of three years plus for the proper placement of structures inside the fort. The projected end result is a Living Historic Park and Museum. Plans are every year, early December at the same time for a re-enactment to occur. A lecture series includes the Seminole Indians for their energetic part of the fort's history.

The second construction phase plans are to include enlisted men's barracks, two officers' quarter's barracks and one with 22 foot cupola on top, inside the fort. The five year project's cost is estimated to be $5 million to $6 million. Educational programs are expanding to match one of the most important military outposts during the removal of the Florida Indians. Fort King was named after Colonel William King who commanded the Fourth Infantry.

You can walk the 1.2 miles of trails thru the woods and down to the 50 foot drop to Seep Springs. Future plans for the free city park including a period building inside and outside the walls of the fort, a new large Visitors Center, a new entrance and a new parking lot.

Osceola, Resistance Fighter

Currently, there is much information on the Fort King Web Page: http:fkha.org/ or www.fortkingocala.com

Fort Mose Historic State Park

St. Augustine, Florida 32084
St. Johns County
National Landmark 1994

The writer holds a new image for you to contemplate. You will not observe these events in our history books. Fort Mose is a symbol of Black freedom in Colonial America and the first free black settlement in North America. Fort Mose has been recognized for its national significance to serve as a memorial to the history of the United States. "In 2009 the National Park Service named Fort Mose as a forerunner site on the National Railroad Network to Freedom." Black slaves escaped to freedom in Spanish Florida in small groups as early as 1687.

Fort Mose created a multi-layered ethnic influence that was joined by Native American Indians and the Spanish Crown. "Fort Mose was established by the Spanish Crown just" two miles north of St. Augustine in 1738 "for African slaves who had escaped from the English colonies of Georgia and South Carolina. Charles V of Spain had decreed in 1693 that any slaves who fled from the British, Spain's enemy at the time, would be given freedom in La Florida." All runaway slaves received freedom and protection if they converted to Catholicism and agreed to serve the Spanish Militia. Fort Mose allowed for the first line of defense for St. Augustine, offering protection from a British attack from the north. By 1738 there were 100 blacks, including women and children, living at Fort Mose. Their work skills included blacksmiths, carpenters, cattlemen, boatmen, farmers, fishing, hunting and doing odd jobs in nearby St. Augustine.

War between England and Spain broke out in 1740. The British had 170 soldiers and dozens of ships to destroy St. Augustine, capital of Spanish Florida. The ships blockaded the harbor and bombarded the town for 27 days. Fort Mose was one of the first places attacked. The diverse population of blacks, Indians and whites pulled together to save the Spanish capital. Fort Mose was lost but recaptured under the leadership of Captain Francisco Menendez, leader of the black militia. Although Fort Mose had been destroyed during the siege, all Fort Mose residents escaped to St. Augustine and resettled in town for the next decade, until Fort Mose was rebuilt in 1748. Florida remained in Spanish hands for the next 80 years.

Spain acknowledged, Captain F. Menendez as the chief of the free Africans, because he spoke five languages. African, Spanish, English and Indian tongues were all heard at Mose. The diverse Mose community was a place of many languages and cultures. Mose's ethnic diversity society included varied backgrounds representing cultural elements such as folklore, personal ornamentation, religion, music and dance. The European conflicts----, British, France and Spain competed for control of the New World's overseas colonial possessions that relied on African labor. "After the British victory against the French in the Seven Years War, the British took over East Florida (1763) in a related trade with the Spanish. The Treaty of Paris gave Florida to England, and Cuba back to Spain."

The residents of Fort Mose, moved once again, including Captain Francisco Menendez, free blacks and the Spanish Military evacuated to a rough frontier of Matanzas, Cuba to escape being re-enslaved by British colonial forces in 1763.

The British refurbished Fort Mose's simple wooden structures and meager thatched homes, "during their 20 year occupation of

Florida." Spanish returned in 1784, again used Fort Mose as a military outpost. The "Florida Patriots intended to capture Florida for the new United States nation" utilized Fort Mose. They failed. The Spanish demolished Fort Mose in 1812. The marsh land sea grasses grew up and tidal waves obscured the existence of Fort Mose.

Years later, rumors collected in St. Augustine of a free black community. Local property owner and historian Jack Williams suspected Fort Mose was on a 24 acre small marsh island. "This second Fort Mose was rediscovered and identified by a combined study of aerial photographs, ancient maps and archaeological remains." The topographic contour map "showed clearly where the moat's earthen walls and posts that were parts of an interior blockhouse and watch tower of the fort had been, and where a modern creek had eaten away one corner of the fort."

The contour map guided the excavation archaeologists from the University of Florida, Museum of Natural History, curator and chair of anthropology Dr. Kathleen Deagan. "With funding ($100,000) from the state legislature, Deagan and 14 student archeologists excavated the small marsh island, which is about two miles north of the present-day Castillo de San Marcos." Two minor digs occurred in 1968 and another in 1977. The last dig began on January 14, 1986. Dr. Deagan's team located "musket balls, gun flints, buttons, and pieces of glass bottles, clay smoking pipes, pottery, rosary beads and animal bones left over from meals." The diggers contended with bugs, heat and occasional snakes. Dr. Jane Landers of the University of Florida researched the documents that identified 47 men, 15 women, 7 boys and 8 girls lived at the fort. "The villagers built a wooden church inside the fort and attended mass given by a Franciscan priest, who lived in the church."

Blacks experienced an activate role in Florida's Colonial History. Visitors can view the grounds 365 days a year. Museum is open Thursday to Monday from 9 a.m to 5 p.m. and closed Tuesday and Wednesday. The State Park contact number is (904) 823-2232.

FORT SAN CARLOS DE BARRANCAS

Pensacola, Florida
Escambia County

National Landmark 1960

The Pensacola community's master theme is defense. Fort Barrancas originated to protect the United States Navy Yard. The fort was completed in 1844 and built on a high bluff overlooking Pensacola Bay. Defenses included two other separate masonry fortifications to protect Fort Barrances. These were Redoubt Battery located half mile inland, north, to protect the fort on the land side. The other site, 1787 Spanish Battery San Antonio, was located south of Fort Barrancas near the shore side.

Earlier Fort San Antonio assumed the defense of Pensacola, as the first Spanish settlement and the capital of West Florida in 1697. Renovated in 1840, its interior tunnels connected Barrancas to the San Antonio Battery. These three strongholds were developed to protect the Navy Yard. National significant Fort Barrancas represented the defenses at the mouth of Pensacola Bay that were materially strengthened to protect the important naval base.

All remained quiet until the Civil War (1861-1865). Florida seceded from the union in January 1861. Union [Feceral] forces held Fort Pickens on Santa Rosa Island, controlling the month of Pensacola Bay that could be easily be reinforced with supplies from this vantage point. Fort Barrances hac only a small force of 44 officers and enlisted men to protect all the federal property in the Pensacola area. Confederate forces consisted of Florida State Troopers, and 500 Alabama troops held the valuable Navy Yard. Cannon fire was exchanged across the bay between Union forces of Fort Pickens and Confederate forces of Fort Barrances. January 1, 1862, *A History of Florida Forts,* DeQuesada writes, "neither side suffered extensively, Fort Barrancas had its flagstaff shot away and its walls scarred."

Model of Fort Barrancas with the Redoubt Battery in the background.

February 1862, Confederate forces removed all useful machinery, cannons, guns, (large and small) from the Navy Yard and its commissary stores. May 7 they burned the remains, marine hospital, barracks and two small steamers and evacuated north to strengthen other field armies. Union forces re-occupied Fort Barrances, the Navy Yard and Pensacola which remained in Union control for the remainder of the war.

After the Civil War, Fort Barrancas Historic District included the other two forts and remained in limited military service. In 1898 during the Spanish-American War and both World Wars, Fort Barrancas was armed and manned, as stated in the landmark record. The fort served as headquarters for the 13th Coast Artillery in defense of Pensacola Harbor. Radio towers were installed on all three forts for civil defenses. The forts were declared functionally obsolete for military use in 1947, "Forts Barrances and Antonio were restored by the National Park Service at a cost of $1,200,000," states DeQuesada. A museum and visitors center is open to the public. Their contact number is 850-934-2600.

* Note the appendix references records and selected reading references

FORT SAN MARCOS DE APALACHE

148 Old Fort Road
St. Marks, Florida
Wakulla County
National Landmark 1966

With this historic legend, the reader crosses three contrasting names. The Spanish period name is the title-Fort San Marcos De Apalache. The Spanish were allies with the Indians, thus bringing in the Apalache into focus. Britain period retained the Spanish name; however the Americans changed the name to Fort St. Marks. During the Civil War, Confederate forces changed the name to Fort Ward.

The coming of Spanish explorers in roughly 1620 exposed the 7,000 Apalache Indians to deadly diseases, small pox and common cold. The beautiful land where the rivers met became a place of struggle and conflict for the next 400 years. This small peninsula formed by the intersection of two rivers, Wakulla and St. Marks. The classic site was the best possible position for defense and shipping.

The fort served as an important center for trade with the Indians. The town contained a foundry and several mills. The region was an active area for blockade-running and salt production.

Florida often was a target in global conflicts between the European empires, Spain, England, and France. Florida's rule changed hands. The Spanish built two inadequate wooden forts on the San Marcos site. Later the Spanish begun to construct a stone fort at San Marcos in 1739, but the unfinished structure passed to England. The British rule of

Florida lasted only 20 years. English troops occupied the San Marcos Fort from 1763-1769 and the troops returned to St. Augustine. Spanish troops returned in 1787, and all was quiet for 13 years.

Spain lacked the ability to control the Indians by preventing them from making raids from Florida against Americans in the north area. "President Monroe gave U.S Army General Andrew Jackson the task of solving the Indian

problem in the South." To protect Americans settlers in the area, Jackson found it necessary to suppress and crush the Indians by force. Jackson's "intervention into Spanish Florida marked the First Seminole War of 1817-1818," explained author DeQuesada, *A History of Florida Forts*.

General Jackson seized Fort San Marcos and "made it his Indian-fighting headquarters by declaring martial law," states DeQuesada. The fort presented, an ideal place for punishing prisoners of war, disobedient Indians and rebellious Europeans. Jackson executed two British spies that were inciting Indian altercations. He left San Marcos on April 29, 1818, and leaving behind 19 Spanish prisoners who soon died from disease, in all likelihood yellow fever. Spanish troops re-occupied the fort.

Spain ceded Florida to the United States in 1821. The Federal government built a Marine Hospital to care for yellow fever patients and victims. (Today, the museum stands on the foundation of Marine Hospital.)

The fort was abandoned prior to the Civil War in 1861. Confederate forces occupied, strengthened, and renamed the fort, Fort Ward. Fierce Confederate troops prevented Union forces from capturing the Florida capital, Tallahassee. Union forces blocked the mouth of the St. Marks River, but Fort Ward protected towns of St. Marks and Newport. A small Confederate steamer CSS Spray equipped with two cannons, assisted in the area's defense. "In February 1864, two Naval expeditions destroyed the salt works at St. Marks and Goose Creek, together valued at $4 million, states DeQuesada." In March 1865, a larger Union force attempted to capture Fort Ward and St. Marks but were met with defeat at the Battle of Natural Bridge near Newport. Fort Ward and CSS Spray remained in Confederate control till the end of Civil War and both surrendered to Union officers May 1865.

The site lay in a state of neglect when the Florida Park Service began work on plans to develop the site as a state park. The property was acquired by the State of Florida in 1964 to use as a park, visitor center and museum. In the summer of 1965, during a routine archaeological check of a dredge spoil area, they discovered wooden objects in the ditch. Upon close inspection archaeologist discovered the wooden objects were coffins, apparently from the military occupation. From the four coffins, one coffin produced a sleeve button, identical to be the type issued to infantrymen in the United States Army from 1814-1821. Another coffin not torn open by the dragline produced a complete skeleton with an intact brain. Skeletal material analysis indicated the soldier died of terminal syphilis. Other artifacts recovered were six infantry buttons of the same period. The four recovered coffins were buried at the museum's military cemetery on high ground.

The Museum

The well-stocked museum provides interpretative exhibits, artifacts, trails to the highest point and the Confederate powder magazine. You can call 850-925-6216 for more details.

Fort Walton Mound

Fort Walton Beach
Okaloosa County
National Landmark 1964

The Fort Walton Mound is a sacred burial site, mixed with shell middens. Professor Tebeau, in *History of Florida*, writes that new Indian immigrants "changed the culture of West Florida." Burials types changed to Temple Mounds with a ceremonial life and less on the cult of the dead. Tebeau gave Fort Walton-Safety Harbor (more about Safety Harbor in another chapter) as examples of the transformation. Burials were mixed with "shards of pottery, shell dippers, ground stone axes, projectile points and knives."

The projected time frame of the "mound is 50BC - AD100 to about AD 1650 by a succession of Indian cultures," Landmark Record states. Fort Walton site was abandoned around A.D.1500 as were many sites across the south were abandoned. Historians speculate that Indian abandonment relates to the arrival of Europeans in North America.

The mound size is 225 by 175 feet at the base and 12 to 17 feet high. A conflict occurs in the records for the reported mound height. The summit platform on the "temple mound at Fort Walton is 180 by 135 feet, was reached by an earthen ramp on the south size "Today, the earth ramp is replaced by a wooden stair ramp.

Civil War soldiers, 1861, established Camp Walton at the base of the temple mound. They installed a cannon emplacement to guard Santa Rosa Sound and Choctawhatchee Bay, the Narrows. In this process the soldiers dug out a shell mound and discovered antiquity, skeletons and ancient objects. The camp was destroyed by fire from Union troops and the relics were lost.

Temple site at the top of the Mound

This archaeological site was investigated and excavated by 11 individuals; some were archaeologists, others were officials to write reports. Many reports were subjective, based on unknown elements of Native American achievements. Dr. C. Fairbanks, Dr. C. Moore, John McKinnon and S.T. Walker were among the first excavators. Other investigators were G. Willey, R. Woodbury, W. and Yulee Lazarus, R.J. Fornaro, and Nina Thanz. N. Thanz investigated the flat surface for the temple building construction, to ascertain if the structure would not disturb any human remains. Previously, other middens around the mound area were covered by modern construction.

"The mound and adjacent Indian Temple Mound Museum are owned and operated by the City of Fort Walton Beach," the landmark record states. Museum's contact phone number is 850-833-9595. The Fort Walton Beach Heritage Park and Cultural Center includes Camp Walton Schoolhouse Museum, utilized for community children from 1912 to 1936. The Heritage Park contains the Garnier Post Office Museum, which is an original small rural post office displaying the postal history of Fort Walton Beach. In 2010 the Heritage Park features the Civil War Exhibits that displays Florida's history during the Civil War.

FORT ZACHARY TAYLOR

KEY WEST, FLORIDA
MONROE COUNTY

NATIONAL LANDMARK 1973

"Fort Taylor helped the United States become a world power," affirmed in the Florida Division of Historical Resources file for military significance. The military significance of Fort Taylor prevailed doing the Civil War, the Spanish-American War, World War I, to a lesser degree World War II and the Cuban Missile Crisis. Key West Naval Station was the most important base in the nation during the Spanish-American War. Fort Taylor defended the strategic harbor for over a century and was the justification for the National Historic Landmark designation.

"The most important naval base during the Spanish-American War" and Fort Taylor defended the Key West Naval Station. The North Atlantic Squadron flagships-- New York, Iowa, Indiana, Oregon and Maine--- under the command of William Sampson were stationed in Key West. "The U.S.S. Maine left Key West for Havana harbor on January 25, 1898, and was blown up." To prevent the invasion of United States by a foreign power, the remaining flagships blocked the Santiago harbor. The Spanish Admiral Cervera had his fleet destroyed at Santiago, thus ending the war on July 3, 1898. The results gave independence to Cuba and the acquisition by the United States of the Philippines and Hawaii.

Lives lost from the war effort were 379 men. "Disease was the great killer in the

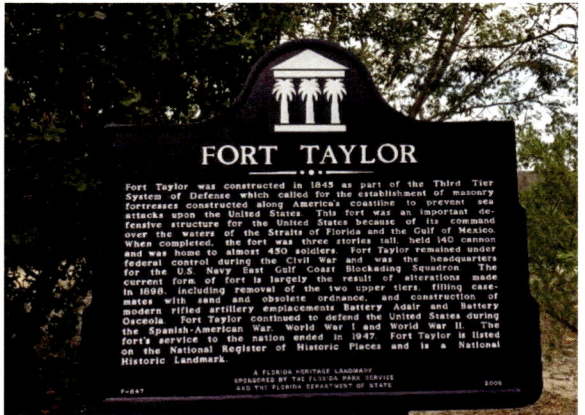

Spanish-America War," and occurred after the fighting had stopped. Grand total lives lost, 4,784, from disease: typhoid fever, camp overcrowding, water contamination, infections due to latrines and garbage pits closeness and lacking camp sanitation. Doctors lacked training or experience in military medicine. The defensive role of Fort Taylor diminished after the Spanish-American War.

A trapezoid structure, three sides facing

seaward, Fort Taylor was built between 1845 and 1866 and guarded the entrance to Key West and the Gulf of Mexico for over a century. During the Civil War, 1861-65, Forts Taylor, Jefferson and Pickens, "held as three federal fortifications that were never seized by Confederate forces," in southern territory. While the fort was still under construction, the fort's 50 ten-inch Rodman cannons, capable of firing three miles, arrived. These fortifications prevented the Confederate Navy from attacks, thus protecting the Navy Base and the island of Key West.

In 1898-1904, Fort Taylor was "modernized" by the Army. The fort's height was lowered to the second-floor level. The razing purpose was for newer weapons installations, such as rapid-fire guns and to replace the original, obsolete 1898 cannons. Old equipment served as infill for the new building modifications. Excavations uncovered the fort's cisterns system, with the largest cisterns underneath the kitchen area. Cisterns were expected to be "adequate for securing the water supply but was aided shortly by the installation of a desalting (desalination) plant." The desalination plant patent specification were secured from the British Museum by Dr. Normandie, a Frenchman.

Years passed, Fort Taylor was re-activated for World War I, 1917-18, for coastal defense operating at sea. Submarines were the new war weapon. A large submarine basin was built just north of the fort. These submarines and patrol vessels fanned out in all directions, watching for enemy operations on the nearby seas. The status of the Naval Station faltered between the World Wars, later was re-established as a significant role in submarine defense.

"Fort Taylor played less of a strategic role in World War II," 1941-45, "as the widespread use of combat aircraft and aircraft carriers had rendered any type seacoast fortification obsolete." Anti-aircraft guns were mounted on the fort's top barrack wings. Radar, machine guns and other devices took the place of cannons. The fort was utilized for training. Two years after World War II ended, the Army turned Fort Taylor over to the Navy for maintenance. During the Cuban Missile Crisis, Key West was the closest observation post for the United States. Fort Taylor was called into action, as a close antenna to track missile installation.

Fort Taylor was designated a National Historic Landmark in 1973. President Zachary Taylor (1850) would be so pleased to have the fort named after him. President Taylor greatest contributions to this country was being a soldier for 40 years. Taylor defeated the Seminole Indians at Lake Okeechobee, Florida on December 25, 1837. The victory gave him the honorary rank of brigadier general. His triumphs in the Mexican War 1847 made Taylor a national hero. He died in office as President after 16 months.

The federal government deeded the fort to the State of Florida in 1976, now under the management of the Florida Park Service. The fort's glory days have passed and serves as a tourist attraction now. Annual fort events include "week-long Civil War reenactments during Halloween. The fort transforms into a haunted house on a grand scale, reflecting a Civil War theme."

*Note the appendix references and selected reading references.

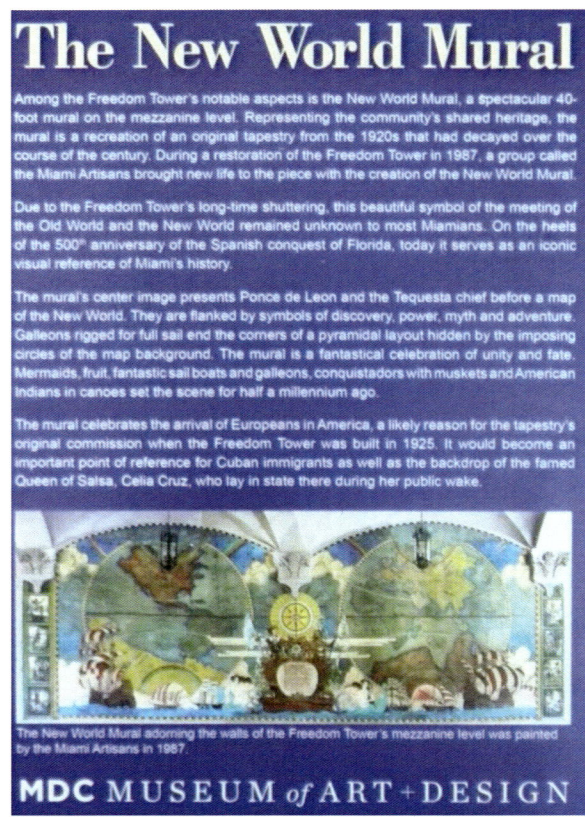

FREEDOM TOWER

600 Biscayne Boulevard
Miami, Florida
National Landmark 2008

The open door welcomes you to Miami Dade College, Museum of Art + Design Museum. Their hours are Wednesday to Sunday from noon to 5 p.m. Admission is free. Phone contact information is 305-237-7700. You can take another look at the beautiful, rare Frieze Architectural design around the amazing front door and columns.

Freedom Tower is referred to as the "Ellis Island of the South." Freedom Tower served as an immigration port of entry and reception center for Cuban refugees from 1962 to 1974. A spectacular icon, Freedom Tower was also known as a gateway to freedom, a beacon of hope, and a monument of liberty.

The stunning Freedom Tower building comprises a four-story base, supporting a twelve-story tower that terminates in an elaborate crown. The building actually possesses a basement story, unusual in South Florida. The captivating center entrance consists of a two-story round arched portal that is embellished with an elaborate pediment, and ornament above; it rises to the height of the four-story base. The fenestration is nine bays wide, and three bays deep. The building is over 82,000 square feet; each of the tower floors (four through twelve) are 1,600 square feet.

In 1925, construction cost was a phenomenal $2 million according to the Miami Daily News. Inspiration for the building's design is based on "The Cathedral" in Seville, Spain. The bell tower begins at the 14th floor and is setback from that point on the plane of the tower section. A terrace creates the base of the 15 and 16 stories, acting to build a crescendo to the crowning cupola.

Architectural style is an eclectic mix of Spanish and Italian elements with an embellishment of Moorish adornments. The eclectic mix of styles occurs in South Florida and often translates to a Mediterranean

Revival style. Other sources describe the mix of styles as "Spanish Renaissance." New York City Architects S. Fullerton Weaver and Leonard Schultze designed the building. This architectural partnership also designed the Miami Biltmore Hotel with a similar appearance.

The site was originally called the Miami Daily News Tower and was constructed to house the offices and printing plant of Miami's first and oldest newspaper.

Newspaper publisher James Cox built the 17-story tower in 1925; it was one of the tallest, 283 feet, buildings in the Southeast. The three-story rectangular building that extends perpendicularly from the tower was built to house the presses. The newspaper building survived the devastating 1926 hurricane and the collapse of the real estate market. By 1928, Miami ceased to flourish. The *Miami Daily Newspaper* endured, and remained at the tower until 1957, when a new plant was constructed. The paper was renamed *Miami Herald*.

The newspaper's use of the tower ended; the tower stood vacant for five years. In April 1962, the building was leased by the United States Government, General Services Administration, to use as the Cuban Refugee Center for immigration. The structure was renamed "Freedom Tower." More than 450,000 Cuban refugees were registered, but, with the declining number of refugees, the building closed in October 1974.

The Freedom Tower is significant for the National Register of Historic Places and Landmark records for two distinct uses. From 1925 to 1957 the building served as the offices and plant facility for the *Miami Daily News and Metropolis*, the city's oldest newspaper. From 1962 to 1974, the tower functioned as the Cuban Refugee Center.

The fate of the Freedom Tower from 1974 to 2007 remained in doubt. In 1987, a Saudi Arabian consortium purchased the building for $7 million with plans for a luxury office building, and banquet hall. While the

Freedom Tower was unoccupied, the building suffered enormous damage. Vagrants stripped the building of brass stair railings, copper roof, and pipes. All of the systems in the building-air-conditioning, elevators, electrical, fire alarms, and life safety, and mechanical systems- needed

complete replacement. The restored magnificent building reopened at a brilliant black tie event in 1988. In 1992, all scheduled ballroom functions were cancelled due to unpaid bills. The building was placed on the market for $6.5 million.

The new buyer, Jorge Mas Canosa, founder and leader of the Cuban-American National Foundation (CANF) purchased the building in September 1997 for $4.2 million. After his death in 2004, the family sold Freedom Tower to the Pedro Martin family, which proposed a new condominium structure. Preservationists opposed the plan. Martin donated the Freedom Tower to Miami Dade College (MDC) in 2005. The College's long-term plan for the Freedom Tower is its conversion into a Cuban-American Historical Museum. The College's euphoric, invigorating opening occurred in 2011 among great splendor.

Tour guide speaks of the Pedro Pan (14,000) children who proceeded their Cuban Families to the United States from December 1960 to October 1962.

Equally important on the Mezzanine Level is the 1925 New World Mural, (40 foot by 20 foot.) The decomposing mural was discovered behind paneling, during the 1987 restoration. Miami Artisans working from black and white photos refurbished the backdrop that serves as a cultural setting for ceremonies in the Freedom Tower Ballroom. To educate future generations, the third floor occupies an extensive Art Museum, while the upper stories serve as specialty functions and offices. When in Miami, you should feel free to stop by for a photos of the Freedom Tower. You can continue on to the next National Landmark site, Miami Biltmore Hotel, and compare their similar architectural styles.

Night Lighting of Freedom Tower

GONZALEZ-ALVAREZ HOUSE

St. Augustine, Florida
St. Johns County
National Landmark 1970

The structure at 14 St. Francis Street is believed to be one of three, Oldest House's in St. Augustine. Documentation is sparse because many real estate records from the First Spanish Period were destroyed by fire. "Puente map of 1764 shows a building on the

site of the Oldest House, owned by Tomas Gonzales Hernandez, a Spanish soldier born in 1701 in the Canary Islands, who had served in Florida since the 1720s," Historic Record states. Years passed and there were several owners at 14 St. Francis Street, but conflict for the oldest house persisted.

St. Augustine Historical Society approached the topic of "conflicting claims of antiquity." After a prolonged discussion, the executive committee resolved the conflict and released the following statement. The committee "cannot positively determine which is the oldest house in St. Augustine, but it is of the opinion, based upon the findings of this committee, that the house known as the Gonzalez-Alvarez house on St. Francis Street, is such," Historic Record states. A year later, in 1918, the Historical Society purchased the Gonzalez-Alvarez house on St. Francis Street.

In a few years the Society purchased the other competing oldest house on St. George Street. The other competing oldest house on Aviles Street (Hospital) was leased, henceforth there would be only one "Oldest House in St. Augustine," Historic Record states. When you tour St. Augustine, go to the Oldest House to inspect the Spanish and English architectural periods.

The Gonzalez house dates back to 1723. The Spanish design is shaped by the living conditions in Florida and building materials

available. Thick walls provide cooling insulation from the Florida sun in this two-room structure. The base of the structure still stands today, a coquina limestone foundation. The detached kitchen is across the court yard in a separate outbuilding. Purpose was to reduce the heat in the house and avoid a fire threat. Today, the kitchen outbuilding is filled with spices utilized by Spanish, and British owners. Gonzalez family left for Cuba in 1763 when the British acquired Florida, under the Treaty of Paris.

The house sat vacant for eleven years, in 1774 Englishman, Major Joseph Peavett purchased the property. Major Peavatt doubled the size by adding a second story, "frame construction with clapboard siding." The hipped roof on the west end where a chimney and fireplace were added at the rear corner. The interior shutters or "rejas" were removed and replaced with "double hung, glazed glass windows" and solid exterior shutters added. Peavett improved the property until his death in 1786.

In 1783 the second Spanish occupation commenced, the Alvarez family from Spain acquired the property in 1790. The family enlarged, improved and held possession until 1882. Afterward the site passed through four other owners. The William Duke family acquired the property in 1882 till 1884, Dr. Charles and Mary Carver from 1884 till 1898, James Henderson family in 1898 till 1911, and South Beach Alligator Farm family 1911 till 1918 and to the present owner, St. Augustine Historical Society. Soon after the Historical Society acquired the house in 1918, the Society was surprised to learn the roof leaked. Inside valuable artifacts were threatened by rain leaking through worn shingles, so the old roof was discarded.

The Oldest House at 14 St. Francis Street has a dual significance. First, it is one of a small number of surviving buildings from the colonial period in St. Augustine. Second, as a popular tourist attraction for the past century, it may be considered a forerunner of modern Florida's biggest industry," Historic Record states.

GOVERNOR STONE

Panama City
St. Andrews Marina
Bay County
National Landmark 1991

October 22, 2017, the Governor Stone members will celebrate the schooner's 140th birthday at the Historic St. Andrews Marina. A National Historic Landmark brass plaque provided by the National Park Service will be presented and installed on the ship. "Governor Stone is the last known survivor in a class of vessels, once numbering in the thousands "and distinctively placed on the National Historic Landmark list, as a working museum. The public is welcome to come on broad this working museum for a 2 ½ hours sailing trip, offered the second Saturday of each month, weather permitting. You can contact Friends of Governor Stone, Info@governorstone.org or call 850-621-0011 for an appointment.

A large sailing ship, the typical schooner has only two masts, with the main mast located toward the center and the shorter mast toward the front. Schooners worked in different environments, from ocean voyages to coastal runs. Schooners required only small crews used for coastal runs and in the fishing trades. These vessels were handy, economical and easily build of accessible materials. Schooners were the errand boys, short haul freighter, the passengers buses and pickup trucks for many a year and contributed to the development of coastal community life. These schooners sailed the coasts in an era before the advent of good all–weather highways made land transportation practical year-round. The schooner Governor Stone was built in 1877 in Pascagoula, Mississippi, for Charles Greiner, as a cargo freighter for his chandlery (storeroom for candles and chandeliers) business. Greiner's good friend was John Marshall Stone, the first elected Governor of Mississippi after the Civil War, thus the name "Governor Stone." Stone's all wooden ship overall length is 63 feet. The single-decked centerboard schooner is 39 feet long at the waterline. "The masts are longleaf yellow pine, rising 38.8 feet from the forestep to the truck and 39.8 feet from the main step to the truck." The mainmast height is 52 feet from the waterline to the topmast. Stone was first outfitted with a 16 HP engine in 1923, but the motor was replaced with a 110 HP Chrysler Marine in 1947. A teak wheel was added in the 1940s.

The yacht led a scintillating 140 year old history with multiple-owners. Second owners, Nathan Mulford Dorlon and Patrick Burns operated the watercraft as an oyster buy boat, by visiting the oyster tonger's while working and taking their catch to market. N. "MUL" Dorlon had a prominent reputation for "doing in the last Gulf Coast pirate, Spud Thompson." At age 69 N.M Dorlon purchased the Stone for $425, soon tired of oyster trade and passed the trade to his partner, Patrick Burns. P. Burns trained his son, Thomas, to captain the ship as a buy boat. "During Prohibition Thomas Burns added a 16 HP motor to the vessel and augmented his oyster buying income by bringing ashore rum shipments from Cuba for $500 a trip." He eluded capture by the Coast Guard. T. Burns operated the craft for 33 more years after surviving two storms. By 1939 the age of wooden schooners had passed. Destiny saved the Stone. Isaac Rhea of Pass Christian,

1942" and it served as a Navy training vessel during the war years. Later, the ship was returned to Rhea in 1947 with a "110 HP Chrysler Marine engine installed". John Curry purchased the craft in 1965. Stone is now a private yacht with modern conveniences.

The Curry family lived on the boat, learned to sail, researched in libraries for Stone's history and interviewed people who remembered her past and became exceptional owners. Curry "funded a restoration that made her a cargo freighter Mississippi was seeking a ship for his luxury resort and rebuilt the Stone top to bottom, but renamed the ship "Inn by the Sea". She carried tourists from 1940 to 1953. The "U.S. War Commission purchased the vessel for $1.00 in

once more, all frills gone except the convenient head and 80 HP Perkins engine". In 1991 Curry donated the vessel to Apalachicola Maritime Institute and Museum in Florida. The schooner became part of Eden Gardner State Park in 2003 but shallow waters did not permit docking. After several stops she was towed to the Fort Walton Beach Marina.

In 2014, Governor Stone was moved again to her permanent home at St Andrews Marina in Panama City. Restoration again refreshed Stone to her former schooner

glory. Additional benefits of sail covers protect the masts from the rains, wind, and sun in the hope of a long future. Governor Stone is the sole known wooden schooner survivor in the American South that sails the Northern Gulf Coast. Today, Stone represents maritime heritage as a floating museum devoted to educational programing historic and cultural tourism.

You, the public are welcome to come on board for a sailing trip in the Gulf on this National Historic Landmark vessel. Sail into the sunshine on tour for 2 ½ hours, offered the second Saturday of each month, weather permitting. You can contact Friends of Governor Stone, 850-621-0011 or Info@governorstone.org for an appointment. You are advised to arrive at the docks by 9:30 and be dressed for sailing weather. The sailing vessel will leave the harbor promptly at 10 a.m. CENTRAL TIME.

HEMINGWAY, ERNEST HOUSE

Key West, Florida
Monroe County
National Landmark 1968

Ernest Hemingway's haunting memory still lives in Key West, spawning reports of apparitions of "Papa" Hemingway all around the island. In 1981, Sloppy Joe's Bar began hosting the annual Hemingway Look-Alike Contest with a weeklong celebration honoring him as a writer and sportsman. In mid-July each year, customers pack the bar to watch cheerful bearded men compete for the title of the Hemingway Look-a-Like Contest. Former Hemingway winning "Papas" judge their worthiness, as hundreds of spectators cheer on their favorites.

Papa Hemingway friends, called "The Mob," are passionately associated with Joseph Russell, owner, of Sloppy Joe's Bar. Hemingway called Russell, "Josie Grunts," and used Russell, as a model for his fictional character Freddy, the owner of Freddy's Bar, and captain of the "Queen Conch" in the novel, *To Have and To Have Not,* which he wrote in 1937 from his life experiences in Key West.

A colorful, disciplined writer, Hemingway was awarded the Pulitzer Prize in fiction for his novel *The Old Man and The Sea,* in 1953. A year *later*, Hemingway won the Noble Prize in literature for *To Have and Have Not.* Hemingway's literary accomplishments bestow significance to the Spanish style house-museum, where he wrote many books.

You should be certain to observe ALL, 3100 structures in 190 block area--the other homes in this Key West Historic District.

Hemingway's literary output while he lived in Key West is difficult to verify. He worked on the following books, in one stage of completion or another: *Death in the Afternoon, God Rest You Merry Gentlemen, Winner Take Nothing, Green Hills of Africa,* and *To Have and Have Not*. In his productive Key West years, Hemingway may have finished *A Farewell to Arms*, and worked on *For Whom the Bell Tolls*. Two famous short stories written from Key West were *The Snows of Kilimanjaro,* and *A Way You'll Never Be.*

Hemingway's disciplined working habits included rising with the sun and working until noon if the words flowed. He always wrote standing up, using the top of a bookcase as a desk in the loft of his pool-house. His royal family of cats surrounded him; their descendants still welcome visitors today. Hemingway often napped in the afternoon, priming himself for companionship at Sloppy Joe's Bar with his drinking buddies.

Hemingway's public persona was shaped from his globe-trotting travels in Spain, Africa, France, and Cuba. His cultivated image was shaped from venues of bullfighting, big game hunting, and deep-sea fishing. Hemingway's father taught him to value the outdoor life, using guns, and being fearless. His mother taught Hemingway culture, by escorting him to art galleries, concerts, and operas. His close friends insist that Hemingway was shy and sensitive.

The Hemingway family acquired one of the older homes in Key West, constructed by Asa Tift in 1854, on a one-acre site. The large two-story, Spanish house made of native

limestone with a flat roof, shutters, wrought iron balconies on three sides. The house is surrounded on all sides by a two-story veranda, with floor to ceiling windows and doors on all sides. In late 1938, he built the first swimming pool in Key West, a 65-foot long concrete pool costing $20,000. The property has a garage with a furnished apartment on the second floor.

The Hemingway's lived on Whitehead Street from 1931 to 1940. He lived there with his second wife, Pauline until 1940 when they separated. Pauline received 51 percent ownership of the Key West property, and continued to live in the house until her death in 1950. The sons did not desire to live in the house so the family rented the property, and owned the property until 1961.

Today, the Spanish style home on Whitehead Street is a museum and opens to the public. Everyone is invited to come to Key West for a charming and refreshing vacation.

HOTEL PONCE de LEON

St. Augustine, Florida
St. Johns County

National Landmark 2006

Floridians are favored! Henry Flagler's first Florida winter visit was in 1877, with his ailing wife Mary. After Mary's passing, he returned to St. Augustine in the winters of 1883 and 1884. He noted the pleasant climate but accommodations were unappealing. His reflective mind pondered the possibilities. Someone with sufficient means ought to "provide accommodations for the class of people who are not sick, but who come here to enjoy the climate and have plenty of money, but could find no satisfactory way of spending it." Flagler's dream of building the "American Riviera, the Winter Newport in St. Augustine," commenced.

Flagler's fortune came from his millions earned as an original partner with John D. Rockefeller, founder of the Standard Oil Company in 1870. Standard Oil became the world's first and greatest oil giant. The daily oil business became routine and Flagler's interest diminished. He remained a vice-president until 1908 and a member of the Board of Directors until 1911.

Flagler's lavish, monumental, palatial first hotel, the Ponce de Leon was built for Gilded Age patrons and has exceptional significance in American architecture and engineering. He selected two brilliant, young (in their twenties) architects, John M.

Carrere and Thomas Hasting, who learned their innovative design principles at Ecole Superieure des Beau-Arts in Paris. Carrere and Hasting employed a significant transforming construction technique. This was the first use of poured concrete in a multistory building in the United States. The concrete mixture consisted Portland cement, sand, and crushed locally quarried coquina shells from Anastasia Island and was applied to all footings, foundations, and exterior walls. Flagler hired local builders, James A McGuire and Joseph A. McDonald.

The first hotel was wired for electricity (with gas lamps as a backup), a system designed by Thomas Edison with 4,100 functioning lights.

Flagler and his architects spared no expense, nor overlooked any details in creating the distinguished palace, in a dazzling design of Spanish Renaissance style embellished with strong Moorish elements. The central block holds several significant features, reflecting its Spanish Renaissance style: a prominent arched entrance with heavy carved doors (5 inches thick); a center dome; and square towers flanking the central block, adjacent to the side wings.

The building's most ornate features are picturesque square twin tower spires, rising 165 feet--notable landmarks on the St. Augustine horizon. These towers were water storage holding tanks (8,000 gallons each), providing water for hotel guests. Brick chimneys rise above the roof line from all points on the four-story structure. The original hotel building occupies an entire city block (7.5 acres) in downtown historic St. Augustine.

The King Street front entrance includes a semicircular paved plaza surrounded by a low concrete fence. The terra-cotta round arch holds an iron and wood portcullis that was raised during the winter season.

Tiffany's Stained Glass Window

A bronze statue of Flagler stands in the entrance. Guests enter a large square courtyard of tropical shrubs and palm trees, with a circular water-spouting fountain of terra-cotta frogs and turtles. A circular walkway around the perimeter of the courtyard leads directly to the hotel entrance. North-south winged building functions to enclose the courtyard.

The main entrance to the hotel proper is directly in line with the south gate. Huge carved double doors surrounded by decorative terra-cotta tile lead into a large foyer and then into the rotunda. The three-story central dome, the rotunda over the lobby, stands out on the horizon. East of the rotunda is reserved space for telegraph office, smoking room, library, reading room, barber shop, and ladies' billiard room. West of the rotunda, a Grand Parlor still exhibits art work by Heade, Ruffio, and Koppay that Flagler purchased to decorate his monumental hotel. The main building, originally designed for 450 guest rooms, is the primary and largest component of the hotel complex. Each guestroom contained a fireplace with wooden mantels with winged cherub faces of inlaid tile.

Henry Flagler engaged the best skilled, world--renowned artisans for his "Flagship" hotel's interiors. The inner canvas walls and ceilings were painted by Virgilio Tojetti, an Italian-born New York artist. Italian craftsmen were brought in to lay the tile, with red marble imported from South Africa and mahogany from Santo Domingo. Records state, that L.A. Tiffany functioned as the decorator. A noted New York design firm, Pottier and Stymus, supplied furniture for the hotel and the rotunda.

Great Dining Room

The magnificent two-story "Great Dining Room" is the hotel's largest public room and is generally considered the most extraordinary and notable. The main hall, 90-feet square, receives natural light for Louis C. Tiffany's 40 stained glass clerestory windows along the side walls of the 48-foot barrel-vaulted ceiling. (This room features 40 of the 79 Tiffany's stained glass windows found throughout the building.) Muralist painter George Maynard, whose work adorns the Library of Congress, is imaginative with whimsical ornamental figures painted on the dining room ceiling. On the north and south walls, Maynard featured "painted ships similar to the ones that carried Ponce de Leon and the French Huguenots ... to the New World."

Tiffany's Stained Glass Dining Room Window

Transportation for Flagler's northern hotel guests was crucial to the success of his resort hotel. Unreliable steamboats only reached coastal cities. In December 1885, Flagler bought interests in the Jacksonville, St. Augustine and Halifax River Railway and linked the line. He built a depot a short distance west of his Hotel Ponce de Leon. In 1889, his railroads provided service from Jacksonville to Daytona, a 90-mile line. This striking, improved transportation increased tourism. In 1889, the system was renamed Florida East Coast Railway. Flagler's future line from Jacksonville to Key West, our southernmost city, extended for a total of 522 miles down the Florida east coast and linked to his luxury hotels. Railroad tycoon Flagler accomplished this task in 24 years.

Upon the completion of the Ponce de Leon in 1887, Flagler's commitment to its success would be accomplished by the improved railroad system. His marketing approach was to mail out thousands of copies of *Florida, the American Riviera*, thus making certain that the world was acquainted with new developments in St. Augustine. During the next years, the Ponce was visited by five presidents, congressmen, and many influential Northerners. In 1888, the hotel's building time took a rapid pace of 18 months; costing $2,500,000. Today, value factors equate the cost to $60 million. Flagler financed this venture out of his own wealth.

The hotel's success as a tourist resort was short-lived for a number of reasons. The yellow fever epidemic kept tourists away from the state in 1888. Florida was hit by the worst freeze in its history in December 1894 and January 1895. The weather was simply not pleasant and sunny, as in the more tropical southern part of the peninsular. Flagler's entrepreneurial enterprises bolted south to Palm Beach, thus ending his dream of turning St. Augustine into the "Newport of the South."

Flagler's accomplishments in St. Augustine were followed by construction of two other hotels, Alcazar, now Lighter Museum and Casa Monica, converted to the St. Johns County Courthouse in 1965. When he arrived few Protestant churches existed Flagler built two churches, Memorial Presbyterian Church (1890) and Grace Methodist Church. Flagler passed in 1913, interred beside his first wife, Mary, and his daughter Jennie at Memorial Presbyterian Church.

Completion of Hotel Ponce de Leon and Flagler's other St. Augustine projects catapulted the young architects, Carrere and Hastings into national prominence. They established their own firm and designed more than 600 structures: New York Public Library, New York City (1911); Russell Senate Office Building, Washington, D.C.(1908); Henry Flagler's House, Whitehall(1901); Cannon House Office Building, Washington D.C.(1908); and more.

Flagler's heirs continued the hotel operation for 79 years and specifically chose adaptive reuse, to preserve the historic hotel and grounds. Henry Flagler's grandnephew, Lawrence Lewis, Jr., founder of Flagler College, envisioned the college as a memorial to Flagler. The continuity of ownership and operations are significant factors in the hotel's preservation.

Flagler College opened in the former hotel in 1968, without significant alterations to the building, however in 1975, a restoration program was launched, proceeding with the least amount of disruption. The original 450 guest rooms were rehabilitated to become 300 dormitory rooms with 150 bathrooms. The towers, Grand Parlor, Dining Room and the Rotunda were restored between 1978 and 1995. In 1981-1982, the former service building, now known as Kenan Hall, provided the college with modern classrooms, faculty office space, computer labs, and the library. Tiffany's 11 Florentine crystal chandeliers still hang in the library, the former parlor.

Fire safety modifications, including fire escapes, were added at the southeast and southwest corners of the hotel building. Ramps for the handicapped were added along the courtyard west wall in keeping with the Secretary of Interior Standards for Rehabilitation. Air Conditioning was added in the dormitory room in 2001. The hotel's two hydraulic-powered elevators (for passengers and luggage) were converted to electric power.

This year Flagler College celebrates the 125th Anniversary of the Ponce (www.Ponce125.com or call 904-829-6481). From January 12 to December 31, 2013, the Legacy Exhibits will illustrate the hotel's construction, art, and the transition to Flagler College (www.flagler.edu., call Marie Coppola, 904-312-3321 or marie@coppolapr.com). You will enjoy a trip to our ancient city which still retains our European heritage in architecture and history. After your exciting visit, you can drive South on I-95 to our nation's only space launching capital--Kennedy Space Center/Cape Canaveral a National Landmark!

HURSTON, ZORA NEALE HOUSE

Fort Pierce, Florida
St. Lucie County
National Landmark 1991

Folklorist, Cultural Anthropologist, novelist, short story writer, and journalist Zora N. Hurston's experienced the world as her laboratory--conducting research and writing. The historical significance statement reads, "Hurston was granted honorary doctorates, published in national magazines, featured on the cover of the *Saturday Review,* invited to speak at major universities, and praised by the *New York Herald Tribune* for being 'in the front rank' not only of black writers, but of all American writers. She was the most important collector of Afro-American folklore in the country. She published more books than any other black American woman."

Alice Walker, author of *The Color Purple,* discovered her house in Fort Pierce, Florida, where Hurston lived at the end of her life, 1957 to 1960. A. Walker credits Hurston for being a genius. Walker revived Hurston's major works, which after their original publication in the 1930s, fell into obscurity. Even with financial hardships she followed her own road, pursued her own dreams, authored ten books, and wrote 50 short stories. Her most successful book (1937),

Their Eyes Were Watching God, was produced for film by Opal Winfrey's Harpo Productions in 2005.

Dr. C. Benton, a family friend from her Eatonville, Florida, childhood, offered Hurston the Masonry Vernacular house, a small two-bedroom home at 1734 School Court, rent free in Fort Pierce, Florida. Benton visited Hurston routinely, only to find Zora did not cook but cultivated her writings. Benton took her to his large home where she would eat with his family. Characteristically, the Eatonville community nurtured her young confidence during her formative years and again in her later years.

State Archives of Florida

Her early life is shrouded in mystery and misreports. Zora birth year is stated as 1891, 1901, 1902 or 1903, as the fifth of eight children. The 1900 census confirms Hurston was born in 1891. Birth place was Notasulga, Alabama. Within a year of Zora's birth, the family moved to Eatonville. Eatonville Historic District is listed in the National Register as the first incorporated black municipality in the

United States--meaning a self-governing town.

Potts, was a country schoolteacher. Hurston loved her mother dearly. Her mother's death shattered her and was a turning point in her 13-year-old life. Her father married immediately. He sent Zora away from her tranquil and favored Eatonville (the setting of numerous writings) and disrupted her education. Her father sent her to care for his brother's children in Jacksonville. Another report stated, that she was sent away to a boarding school in Jacksonville. Her parents stopped paying her tuition and the school expelled her. Possibly at age 15, Hurston was in the world alone! One of her first jobs entailed wardrobe work for the lead singer traveling with a Gilbert and Sullivan Company. At age 26, in 1917, Zora began modifying her birth date, apparently to qualify for a free education.

She attended and graduated from Morgan Academy in Baltimore, Maryland.

In 1918, she matriculated at Howard University, Washington D.C. Hurston co-founded the University's student newspaper, *The Hilltop.* Her four years at Howard mark the beginning of her writing career in the 1920s. Hurston achieved success in writing contests, college publications, newspapers, and magazines. Courses completed were Spanish, English, Greek, and Public Speaking; she earned an Associate's Degree in 1924.

Hurston relocated to New York City to fulfill her dreams. In 1925, she occupied an award winning role with Harlem

Her father, John, was a carpenter and a Baptist preacher; her mother, Lucy Ann

Renaissance, a black literary and cultural movement. At an awards dinner, Hurston's writings won second prize. Zora introduced herself to novelist Fannie Hurst *Imitation of Life,* 1933 who gave her a job. She also met Annie Nathan Meyer, "who arranged for her to receive a scholarship to Barnard College," a private women's college. In 1925 and 1933 Hurston published *John Redding, Muttsy* and a play, *The First One.*

While she was at Barnard College, Hurston's writings gained the attention of anthropologist Dr. Franz Boas, who was teaching at Columbia University. Inspired by Professor Boas and a $1,400 Fellowship from the Carter G. Woodson Foundation, Hurston was on a mission to collect African-American folklore, customs, superstitions, jokes, dances, and games. Between 1927 and 1931, Hurston's folklore collection centered in Florida and Alabama towns. From her collection work in the south, 1928 to 1932, she produced *Mules and Men* (1935), regarded as a folklore classic. In 1934, she published a successful six-essay *Anthology.* While at Barnard College in 1927, she married fellow student, Herbert Sheen; the marriage was short-lived.

In 1934, Hurston met her goal; she published her first novel, *Jonah's Gourd Vine;* her father was the prototype. The story line is about a Baptist minister who was as a holy man on Sunday but led an adulterous life Monday through Saturday. It was followed by the "classic black literature" her second novel, *Their Eyes Were Watching God*, in 1937. The story is "of a young black women in search of self and genuine happiness."

Her cultural anthropological field work continued out of the country in the Caribbean, Haiti, and Jamaica, supported by a Guggenheim Foundation grant. Her *Tell My Horse* emerged, a study of Caribbean voodoo, in 1938. The late 1930's and early 1940s marked the peak of Hurston's literary career.

In the early War World II years, Hurston was teaching at Florida's Norman College in St. Augustine, Florida.

"She read Marjorie K. Rawlings's *Cross Creek (1942),* which impressed her, and struck up a correspondence with the novelist." Rawlings later assisted Hurston with her publisher, Scribner and they published her next book in 1948, *Seraph on the Suwannee.* Surprisingly, this book applied to white folks that she wrote about while living in Honduras.

Hurston accepted "jobs where she could find them," as a freelance writer, teacher, reporter, librarian, reporter, and maid work. In 1957, she moved to Fort Pierce, where she died in poverty and obscurity from a stroke and heart disease in January 1960. The world still honors the talented, accomplished, prized writer, Zora Neale Hurston of Eatonville, Florida.

INGHAM: U.S. COAST GUARD CUTTER

Truman Park Waterfront
Key West, Florida
Monroe County

National Landmark 1992

This astonishing fifty one year service record of the *Ingham* is celebrated as the most decorated vessel in the Coast Guard Fleet. *Ingham* received two Presidential Unit Citations for extra-ordinary bravery in action against an enemy. The vessel's length of service and eighteen awards received is the justification for the National Landmark designation.

Presently, the *Ingham* is a floating museum exhibit at the Truman Waterfront in Key West, Florida. The ship was transferred to Key West from Patriots Point Naval and Maritime Museum in Mount Pleasant, South Carolina, "due to financial circumstances that restricted the continued maintenance of the vessel." The *Ingham* arrived in Key West on November 24, 2009 in ready condition with manuals, watch bills, equipment, gear and uniforms which give the impression the crew has just stepped ashore.

These coast guard cutters were named for notable Secretaries of the Treasury. Four cutters were launched in 1936 from the Philadelphia Navy Yard. They were George W. Campbell, William J. Duane, Samuel D. Ingham and Roger B. Taney and Alexander Hamilton from the New York Navy Yard and

called "Secretary Class" or "Treasury Class".

From this vessel class only two survive today. *Taney* is a National Historic Landmark in Baltimore, Maryland, recognized for her wartime career in the Pacific and her activity in the Japanese attack on Pearl Harbor. As Commander-in-Chief, the *Ingham* represents the other Coast Guard vessels who engaged in the Battle of the Atlantic war venue.

Ingham is a 327-foot long riveted steel high-endurance cutter, carrying two 5-inch/51 caliber guns. In 1945, *Ingham* was equipped with SC-2 and SGA radar, and QC sonar. "The cutter has four decks: superstructure deck, main deck, second deck, platform deck and four-level superstructure." The main deck accommodates the galley, ship's office, First Class crew's berthing, blower room, engineer's work shop, stores, sickbay, and gear lockers. During the war years the vessel was painted camouflage colors, now repainted white, with the distinctive Coast Guard orange stripe across the bow.

From Port Angeles, Washington, *Ingham* was reassigned working off of the Grand Banks of Newfoundland, working Neutrality Patrols and weather station duty. In July 1941, United States entered World War II conflict, when German U-boats began attacks on American shipping. With a shortage of submarine warfare, the Secretary Class cutters proved most valuable. *Ingham* was assigned Commander-in-Chief of the Atlantic Fleet based out of Iceland, defending seventeen convoys. "I*ngham* engaged in major seagoing battles to defend precious oil, material, and men to war torn Europe." In this war front the *Ingham* sank an enemy submarine U-626. *Ingham's* other notable events were rescuing survivors from six different war ships. The data does not count the exact number rescued, however the count may be well over one hundred saved. As the German U-boats attacks lessened in the Atlantic, the Secretary Class Cutters accomplishments were glorious but casualties were heavy. In mid-1943, *Ingham* was transferred to the Mediterranean convey duty, escorting 12 Mediterranean convoy and two Caribbean convoys and earning the Presidential Unit citation for bravery.

In the summer of 1944, the *Ingham* and the sister cutters served a new role as amphibious communication control ships in the Pacific war effort. *Ingham* spearheaded the liberation of the Philippine territories. After the war, *Ingham* returned to traditional Coast Guard service, search-and-rescue, weather patrol, and law enforcement. In 1968-1969 the cutter returned to combat serving off Vietnam during Operations Market Time, Swift Raider and Sea Lords, earning the Presidential Unit Citation. In 1980 *Ingham* assisted in the Mariel Boatlift rescue operations, saving lives at sea by escorting to two Cuban refugee vessels to Key West.

Ingham was decommissioned on May 27, 1988 as the oldest warship and the most decorated ship in the coast guard fleet. In her fifty-one year career she and her crew racked up an impressive eighteen awards. One award referred to the *Ingham* as the "Guardian of the Sea."

You will see these awards when you visit the vessel in the Key West harbor. For visiting hours you can call this contact number is (305) 292- 5072.

*Note the appendix references and selected reading references

LLAMBIAS HOUSE

St. Augustine, Florida
St. Johns County

National Landmark 1970

"Among the few surviving structures in St. Augustine that date from the first Spanish period, this house reached its final form by 1788. A restored example of organic growth of a dwelling built on a variation of the St. Augustine Plan, which combines English and Spanish architectural details" Historic Record states.

St. Augustine was the first permanent Spanish settlement in 1565. Homes built and designed in this period were created to withstand the hot, humid, turbulent climate of the ocean front city, known for the St. Augustine architecture guidelines. Llambias House, 31 St. Francis Street, the date of construction is unknown. However, the house appears on the 1764 Puente Map listing Pedro Fernandez as the owner. Fernandez constructed a one-story rectangular shaped, one room with coquina-masonry walls. Thick coquina walls provide protection from heat in the summer and the cold in the winter. Kitchen cooking often smoked up the house, but the smoke acted as a mosquito repellent. The main entrance, often, was through the loggia or porch. Fernandez sold the property to Jesse Fish when the Spanish left Florida, the British gained control of Florida in 1763.

From 1764 to 1783 the property transferred to two other owners, R. Henderson then to E. Corbel. In 1783 N. Turnbull acquired the property. "Turnbull was responsible for enlarging the house to a two-story, four-room coquina-masonry building, with a wooden balcony on the second-story façade, a two-story rear masonry- and-wood gallery addition and a masonry chimney," Historic Record states. Turnbull left St. Augustine when Spain gained Florida again, in 1783 and the property reverted back to J. Fish in 1784. After Fish's death in 1790 the property was sold at auction. From 1792–1854, eight new owners acquired the property, M. Morena sold to P. Marrot, to J. Andreu, to his widow, C. Pons, to her daughter, C. Giiraldo and Pons' son in law and the property was sold at auction again.

Captain B. Pierce sold the property in 6 months to Dr. T. Simmons. In 1835 Dr. Simmons sold to Rev. E. Thomas, who later sold to Manucy brothers in three years. J. Manucy sold in 1854 to Catalina Liambias "after whom the house is named" and the property remained in the family for 65 years," Historic Record states. During the Civil War, 1861- 1865, St. Augustine was occupied by the Union forces. Father Llambias refused to take the loyalty oath. Both mother and father left the area. Upon returning after the war, they found the house had been "stripped of its furniture and woodwork, and the ground floor used as a stable," Repairs were made. "In 1877, Catalina Llambias deeded the house to her two daughters", Historic Record states. Two generations of the Llambias family lived in the house until it was sold to H. Campbell in 1919.

Campbell hired a group of men to clean up the overgrowth vegetation on the large lot, 90 x160 ft, (English measurement) to beautify the site. He added a two-story, L-shaped addition on the west side of the rear of the building. In 1932 Campbell sold the property to the Newbill family.

In 1938, the three Newbill sisters sold the house to the Carnegie Institute, which was involved with the preservation program in St. Augustine. Three days later, the Carnegie Institute conveyed the property to the City of St. Augustine.

"The appearance of the Llambias House today is the result of a 1954 restoration by the St. Augustine Restoration and Preservation Association in cooperation with the St. Augustine Historical Society," Historic Record states. In the 1954 restoration, the façade door providing access into the building from St. Francis Street was closed off. New access was created into the courtyard through a wooden gate in the coquina-masonry wall. A small chimney on the east of the house

was removed. Other repairs were completed. "In 2005, the St. Augustine Historical Society resumed its role as custodian of the Llambias House," Historic Record states.

For additional information, such as a tour or to rent the house as a Wedding venue call (904) 824-2872. Few of these centuries old houses still exist today, which makes the Llambias House a very special National Historic Landmark.

MAPLE LEAF

Mandarin Point

St. Johns River

Duval County

NATIONAL LANDMARK 1994

A stimulating Civil War tale. Floridians acted as an uninvolved trader of goods to the Confederate army. Union strategists needed to take Floridians out of the war equation. Union ships blockaded the coastlines and patrolled the St. Johns River. Floridians fought back. "Confederate forces placed mines in the St. Johns River." On April 1 1864 Maple Leaf Ship struck a Confederate torpedo and sank quickly. Four crewmen sleeping on the foredeck were killed instantly, but the remaining passengers and crew escaped into boats and were saved," Historic Record states.

The most significant Civil War Battle fought in Florida was the Battle of Olustee (15 minutes east of Lake City in the heart of designated Osceola National Forest). Union forces sought to gain control over the supply lines from the interior of Florida.

Union forces lost at Olustee and the soldiers returned to Jacksonville. Confederate troops controlled the interior of Florida that was a threat to Union forces.

The Maple Leaf returned from Charleston fully loaded with personal baggage. After the arrival in Jacksonville," the ship's orders were to transport a cavalry unit to Palatka but her freight was not unloaded" the Record states. All soldiers and horses were unloaded in Palatka. However, forty-two northerners and their goods (baggage) came aboard for the trip back to Jacksonville. "In the early morning, 4 a.m. April 1, 1864, the new device, Confederate torpedo, (a keg of 70 pounds of powder) blasted the right side of her hull ---and the Maple Leaf sank quickly," Record states. A portion of the smoke stack remained above the water, but the Confederates burned the Maple Leaf to the water line.

In April 1864, the United States Government stated, everything was lost and not worth salvaging. Government (Army) had clear title to the wreck as lease holders to the ship, but the ship's owners were Bostonians J.H.B Spears and Charles Lang. For their lost, the "owners were awarded compensation of $19,987" Record states.

The Maple Leaf wreck was three decks high and was blocking a portion of the St. Johns River that posed a serious threat to other vessels. A lighted buoy was placed over the wreck. In 1888, R. G. Ross was awarded a contract to remove the vessel but he moved the vessel to another river site. The buoy was removed and the Maple Leaf forgotten.

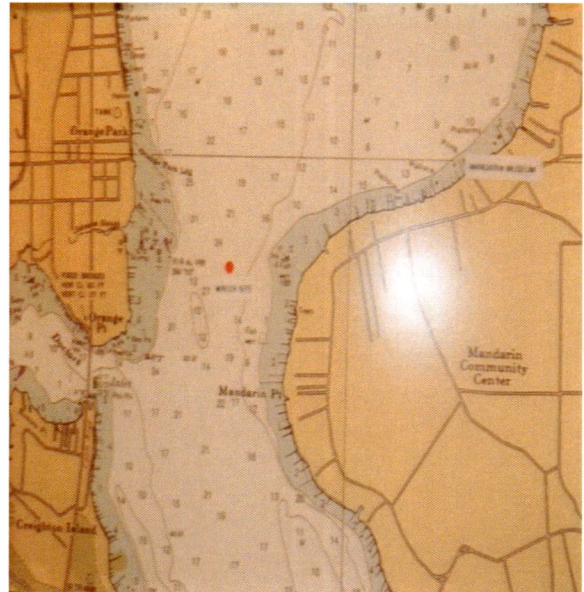

In 1984 Keith Holland, a dentist and part-time archaeologist found the shipwreck off Mandarin Point. The Maple Leaf find became a recovery project but ownership rights were in disagreement. Holland and his diving crew of the St. Johns Archeological Expeditions Inc. began the recovery of 440 tons of well-preserved artifacts. Maple Leaf's promise was to yield much information on military history, practices and nautical architecture.

The first state grant for the recovery project awarded to the Archaeological firm for the divers, was $304,000 and an additional grant of $184,250 was awarded, stated the Jacksonville Historical Society. James Miller, State Archaeologist specified possible preservation techniques for the artifacts. Miller stated, "there is no precedent for what will be required in this excavation and preservation of the artifacts, but the entire cargo is well preserved" Record states.

In August 1984, ownership rights came to the surface for the signing of Landmark Application. The "Army had some doubt as to its role as one of the owners the property. From an Admiralty Court agreement stated the vessel belonged to the Army---and the bottomlands of the St. Johns River where the wreck is embedded, belong to the State of Florida," Barbara Mattick Memorandum, Bureau of Historic Preservation, Tallahassee, Florida. The wreck site is jointly owned by the U.S. Department of the Army and the State of Florida.

Hopefully, readers have a clue from the Maple Leaf name that the ship was Canadian built in 1851 .The ship's purpose was to carry freight and passengers on the Great Lakes. In 1862 the Maple Leaf was leased to the United States Government as an Army transport for the Southeast Atlantic blockade. The ship's dimensions were 173 feet long, 3 decks high, width of 26.5 feet and holding depth of 11 feet or a 508 ton capacity.

Maple Leaf artifacts are on display at the Mandarin Museum. For additional information, you can call the Mandarin Museum, 904-268-0784 in the Walter Jones Historical Park.

Florida Department of State, Division of Historical Resources, Florida Master Site File

State Archives

MAR-A-LAGO

Palm Beach, Florida
Palm Beach County
National Landmark 1980

A seventy-five foot tower tops the structure giving a spectacular view in all directions of the waterways, both the Atlantic Ocean and the Intracoastal Waterway, for miles. Marjorie Merriweather Post, an astute heiress and the founder of General Foods, built the sprawling Mediterranean-style villa that symbolized a wealthy, aristocratic way of life in Florida during the 1920's land boom.

The estate is positioned on perfectly landscaped seventeen acres, with a nine-hole golf course, citrus groves, green houses, cutting garden, guest houses and staff quarters. A stone path leads to a tunnel under South Ocean Boulevard that opens to the beach. To the left on the beach is a private cabana and pool and to the right is the bath and tennis club. Mar-A-Lago's foremost purpose was to serve as a short term, two months of the year a winter vacation playground in a semi-tropical climate. Mar-A-Lago is Spanish and means "Sea to Lake."

Marjorie M. Post selected Architect Marion Sims Wyeth for the exterior design and Joseph Urban for the interior designs. Three boat loads of Dorian stone were shipped from Genoa, Italy, for the exterior walls. To view Wyeth's exterior designs, your best opportunity is an internet search of Mar-A-Lago. Cooper C. Lightbrown of Washington, D.C., received the construction contract.

Skilled workmen from the West Palm Beach area were recruited for work. Urban's Interiors is the living room, the central and most important room, often called the gold room. Urban's adaptations draw on the inspirations from "Thousand-Wing Ceiling" in the Academia at Venice, Italy. Lofty gold-leaf ceilings are almost a lost art because few craftsmen exist to apply the gold paper, but Urban was victorious. Urban's dining room marble table top was inlaid with different semi-precious stones, made in Old Medici Marble Works in Florence, Italy. These are a few of the extraordinary features that appoints Mar-A-Lago as one of America's Treasures, and in 1980 the site was declared a National Historic Landmark.

Marjorie Post began construction in 1923 and it was completed in 1927-- her vision achieved. The estate anchored in stone, concrete, and steel has withstood hurricanes and tropical storms over the years. She had 46 years to winter in Florida, enjoying the ocean breezes. Post passed away in 1973. Her last will and testament transferred the Mar-A-Lago Estate to the federal government to use as a diplomatic or presidential retreat. The costs of maintaining the estate exceeded the funds provided by the Post Foundation. The National Park Service recommended the estate be returned to the Foundation by an Act of Congress April, 1981. The Post heirs listed the property for sale for $20 million; since they expected to sell the property, it was not maintained and the site declined. Businessman Donald Trump offered to purchase the property but the offer was rejected. In 1985 Trump purchased the property, including all the furnishings for $5 million. His intention was to use the property as a single family residence.

Trump renovated and enhanced Mar-A-Lago Estate by adding a Louis XIV- style ballroom, 20,000 square-feet. He modified the total room space from 118 or 126 (from two different sources) down to 58 bedrooms, 33 bathrooms, 12 fireplaces and three bomb shelters. Renovations included five new clay tennis courts. For security reasons, additional tax roll information is not available. Trump confronted financial issues in the 1990's. He planned to subdivide Mar-A-Lago's 17 acres into nine separate lots. These expectations alarmed the Palm Beach Community. The National Register and Landmark records documented 30 pages of records for Design Guidelines, Landscape Guidelines, Appurtenant Structures, Civil Engineering Design Parameters, and a Traffic Study. Palm Beach Preservation Board rejected the subdivision application. After the subdivision replat rejection, Trump turned the estate into a private club and spa, approved by the Palm Beach Town Council. Club membership fees in January 2017 for nearly 500 paying members was $200,000 annually. Fortune.com stated the Club reportedly earned Trump $15.6 million in 2016.

In 2006 Donald Trump erected a 80 foot flagpole on the front lawn with a 15-by-25 foot American flag. Both were over Palm Beach Zoning restrictions, so the town began to fine Trump $250 daily. Total fines arrived at $120,000, so Trump sued for $25 million, claiming an abridgement of his First Amendment Rights of free expression.

Government and Trump agreed to compromise. Trump reduced his flagpole height down to 70 feet and donated $100,000 to veterans' charities. In the end, Trump won this conflict, because he has the tallest flagpole in town!

Over the years Trump has filed several Aviation Litigation against Palm Beach International Airport to change flight patterns because of noise and pollution passing over Mar-A-Lago.

Donald Trump was sworn into office as President of the United States on January 20, 2017. Trump describes Mar-A-Lago as the Winter White House. Marjorie M. Post's objective is met. In the first 100 days of the Trump administration he conducted government affairs from the site on five consecutive weekends. On the second visit, President Trump hosted two international leaders, Japanese Prime Minister Shinzo Abe and on the fourth weekend visit, he hosted Chinese leader XI Jiniping for two days. Air Force One carries the president, his entourage, guests and costs roughly $180,000 per hour. Extra cargo planes packed with motorcade limousines and other equipment are needed. Additional aircraft are needed to transport personnel who conduct security sweeps before the president arrives. Should the president require a helicopter another bigger cargo plane is needed.   These are the many drivers of presidential travel costs. "A trip to Mar-A-Lago costs taxpayers approximately $3.6 million, according to Government Accountability Office report." Security in Palm Beach during these presidential visits are burdensome for the local population. Palm Beach's Lantana Airport is shut down, which accumulates a financial lost for multiple businesses. Coast Guard secures the two waterway approaches, ocean and lake. Traffic is tied up for hours, because Secret Service cordons off streets to Mar-A-Lago for hours. President Trump has requested a helicopter pad be built on the western part of the 17.5-acre Mar-A-Lago property, to avoid stopping traffic on South Ocean Boulevard. Palm Beach's Town Council and National Trust for Historic Preservation may give their approval.

You can drive down 1100 South Ocean Boulevard, Palm Beach for a glimpse of Mar-A-Lago.

MIAMI-BILTMORE HOTEL AND COUNTRY CLUB

1210 Anastasia Avenue

Coral Gables, Florida

Dade County

National Landmark 1996

Countless individuals flying into Miami International Airport ask, can you disclose the name of the elaborate monument? The towering beauty looms above the landscape. It stands 300 feet high, powerful with pride, as the centerpiece of the Coral Gables community. The Miami Biltmore is Coral Gables' most significant reminder of the Florida land boom; it is one of the most prestigious monuments of this era in South Florida and is a National Landmark.

George Merrick's "City Beautiful" vision emerged from a "balanced city" plan, which provided for persons of all classes, and incomes. Merrick used his father's grove as a basis, and accumulated 1,200 more acres. Merrick opened his land sales office, and sold $150 million worth of lots. Unlike other developers, he only had moderate means. However, he had an aptitude for city planning and marketing skills. He utilized his new funds for stylist enhancements— fountains, golf courses, winding canals, a Venetian Pool, and landscaping. Despite the great disadvantage of no ocean front, on November 25, 1924, Merrick announced that John Bowman of the Biltmore Hotel Corporation, agreed to build a $10 million hotel in Coral Gables. The Biltmore name brought credibility, as well as national attention.

Having a national reputation for hotel design, Bowman selected the architectural firm of Schultz and Weaver. The architects' hotel design included a 15-story symbolic core tower, inspired by the famous Giralda Bell Tower Cathedral in Seville, Spain, with seven-story east and west wings extending at an angle in an imposing Mediterranean Revival style. The magnificent entranceway consists of colossal Ionic Columns and above a small enclosed balcony that creates a unified central bay. West of the hotel, Country Club building erected in April 1925, maintains a banquet room on the second floor.

The 19.8-acre grounds contain a bridle path; fox hunting area, two golf courses, a polo field, tennis courts, and Olympic-sized swimming pool with grandstands, where Tarzan's Johnny Weissmuller and others entertained.

The formal opening occurred on January 15, 1926 with a great testimonial banquet honoring John Bowman and George Merrick. To mark the hotel's completion, a 37-hour ride on special trains carried 300 dignitaries from New York for food, drink, dancing, gambling, along with celebrities, wealthy tourists, and residents.

The magnificent hotel's interiors portray a sense of grandeur. Many luxurious features, including lofty ceilings of gold leaf, imported Spanish tiles, mahogany paneling, 26 Corinthian columns in the lobby, medieval fireplaces, chandeliers, antique Spanish furnishing, pink coral rock stairways, and marble floors. Merrick had not overlooked any details.

Gold Leaf Ceilings and Chandeliers

On the fringe of the real estate bust of 1926, Merrick's Coral Gable Corporation declared bankruptcy in April 1929. The hotel and country club transferred to John Bowman and investors. Hotel functions continued under owner Henry Doherty until 1938.

Throughout its colorful 86-year history, the Biltmore has served in numerous capacities, a celebrated winter resort for the socially prominent for 17 years; the undamaged hotel opened as a community shelter for 3,000 during the 1926 hurricane. The hotel's tower served as a secret radio station for aircraft spotters during World War II. War officials requested the hotel turn out its lights, and that contributed to the beginning of the hotel's end.

The federal government later purchased the hotel for $900,000, a tenth of its value, to use as a convalescent hospital with 1,200 beds. Writer Kleinberg stated, "The military dumped valuable antique Spanish furnishings and dinnerware onto the street outside the hotel," and painted over decorative elements. In 1946, they renamed the facility Pratt Hospital; General Dwight Eisenhower was a patient.

Merrick probably witnessed the government's abuse of his jewel; he died of a heart attack at the age of 56 in 1942.

From 1947 to 1968, the Veterans Administration operated the facility; then it was transferred to Jackson Memorial Hospital. The federal government still owed the facility. The Biltmore then became a dog kennel used for medical experiments.

Then citizens campaigned to "Save the Biltmore." In 1973, the federal government transferred the Biltmore to the City of Coral Gables. Committed citizens cleaned it up; the city spent $62 million restoring the Biltmore around 1985 and submitted the landmark application. Hotel room capacity was reduced from 400 to 275 rooms. Still, like a real monument and a true landmark, the Miami-Biltmore endures, reflecting our nation's architectural history and beauty.

MIAMI CIRCLE AT BRICKELL POINT

Miami, Florida

Miami-Dade County

NATIONAL LANDMARK 2009

The picturesque site located on the Miami River is one of discovery. The Brickell Point Site is significant for the identity and frame of reference as a Native American archaeological site. The valuable scientific research and new knowledge was gained from a regionally important Indian village as a political organization. The Brickell Point location was widely visible as it overlooked Biscayne Bay to the east and Miami River to the west.

NPS Form 10-900 USDI/NPS NRHP Registration Form (Rev. 8-86) OMB No. 1024-0018

THE MIAMI CIRLCE AT BRICKELL POINT SITE — Photos

United States Department of the Interior, National Park Service — National Register of Historic Places Registration Form

Florida Department of State
Division of Historical Resources
Florida Master Site File

Photograph 5 of 28. Aerial photograph of Brickell Point and the Miami River, ca. 1918 by Richard B. Hoit. The photograph shows the dredging and bulkheading of the Brickell property on the south bank of the river. The structure shown on the south bank of the river is the rusticated block building built in 1909 by the Brickell family and used as a boarding house. Comparison of this photograph with the image in Photograph 4 demonstrates that the columns in front of the building are simply part of the front porch. Image Rc19618, Florida State Archives, Tallahassee.

The environmental setting occupied by the Brickell Point Site is a 2.2 acre parcel on the south bank of the mouth of the Miami River, where it meets Biscayne Bay. Site is abutted by the Sheraton Hotel to the south including the First Presbyterian Church and the Brickell Avenue Bridge to the west. All are located on the limestone formation Atlantic Coastal Ridge that underlies all of Coastal Miami.

The State of Florida investigated the entire Brickell property, Brickell Park, not just the Miami Circle. The prominent land owners, enterprising, pioneer Miami family, William and Mary Brickell, owned much acreage on Brickell Avenue. Vizcaya's James Deering purchased 180 acres on the coast line in Coconut Grove from the Brickell family. The Brickell Family acquired ten acres in and around Brickell Point, in the time frame of 1871."Brickells established their residence and a general store just south of the mouth of the Miami River," Record states. Tequesta Indians were their customers at the general store. Can we conclude, the Tequesta Indians communicated to the Brickells, that Brickell Park was the scared cemetery grounds of the Tequesta Indians? In 1924 the Brickell Family established an agreement with the City to protect Brickell Park, as downtown Miami rose around Brickell Park. Recently, 2001, Brickell family third generation heirs sold an easement of Brickell Park to the neighboring owners with the City's approval.

May 1998, demolition of the 1950's low-rise Brickell Point six apartment buildings commenced. Dade County Historic Preservation Director, Robert Carr, visited the site to inspect the demolition work, and noted the required archeological monitoring was not being performed. Carr requested a stop work order to the developer, Brickell Pointe Limited. An archaeological consultant was retained by the property developer to monitor ground disturbing activities. Demolition work continued, including the destruction of a below ground swimming pool and basement area, tree removal, and building footings. Excavations preceded from all the Brickell property encountering several alignments of post holes drilled in the limestone. The 38-foot wide circle, with holes pocked in the jagged limestone was discovered in May 1998, where demolition crews prepared to build a high-rise condominiums. Carbon dating suggested that the circle was used Tequesta Native Indians. Archeologist Widmer, Shapiro,

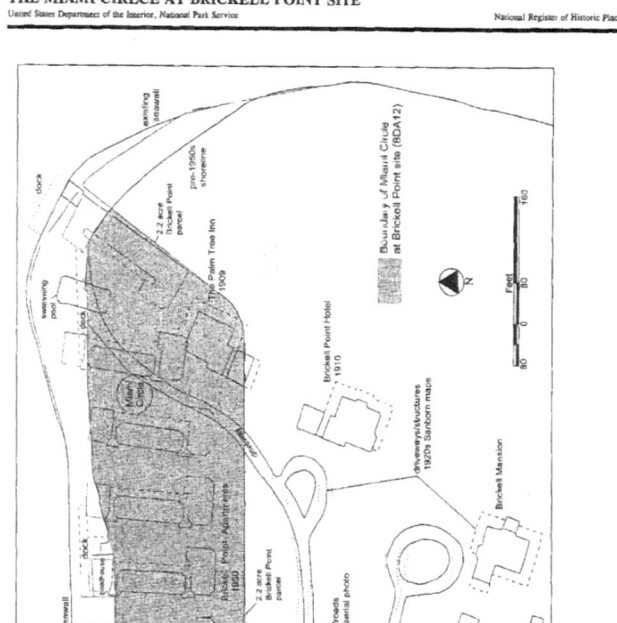

Figure 6. Map by archeologist Jorge Zamanillo showing the footprint of the Brickell family buildings and driveways, as well as the footprint of the Brickell Point Apartments. The archeological deposits of 8DA12 are shown in gray.

Florida Department of State, Division of Historical Resources, Florida Master Site File

McEwan, Weisman (2000) studied "507 posthole features cut in the limestone" and the artifact features. Widmer dubbed the area "Valley of the Holes." Comments from archaeologists disclosed and suggest the Circle is about 2,000 years old and the site served as a native ceremonial center even after Europeans arrived. In November 1999, the Circle was declared authentic by the archaeologists.

"Recent archeological testing of Brickell Park confirmed past observations that this part of Brickell Point Site may contain an American Indian cemetery," Record states. Anthropologist A. Elgart report human bone fragments and teeth were found associated with the Miami Circle located to the south of the site. "A total of 340 historic artifacts were recovered as a result of three phases of archeological investigations at the Miami Circle parcel. Recovered materials are divided into three classes of materials: ceramics, metal, and glass," Record states. These artifacts have a direct historical connection with the Tequesta Indians. 100 artifacts from the now-extinct Tequesta Native Indians are on display (October 15, 2002) at Historical Museum, on Flagler Avenue, and the exhibit is called "First Arrivals." Artifacts consist of skull of a dolphin, upper shell of a turtle-"carapace", copper beads, arrow points, and hand-held tools,(palm-sized axes). Scientific analysis of tools by geologists from the University of Miami stated the axes "were produced hundreds of years ago by people who lived in central Georgia,-- proving that an active, trading civilization existed in South Florida," Record states. Exotic materials, axes and more will be in one place for the public to view.

A large Native American village of the Tequesta Indians indicates that their society was "socio-politically complex." "Archeology confirms that their economy was based on fishing, hunting and gathering, with a reliance on dugout canoes, which were used along the coast and in the Everglades (Glades)", Historic Record states." The Tequesta encountered by Ponce de Leon on his voyage to Florida in 1513," Record states. Alliances were often bonded through marriage. Tequesta Chief was a "near relative" of the Calusa Chief, sometime an ally and sometime hostile." Tequesta persisted for over 250 years, largely due to well-established cultural patterns. Other native groups fell quickly after being exposed to European diseases. "Radiocarbon dates place the Miami Circle and deposits within the Glades I period (500 B.C –A.D. 500) to Glades 1 late (A.D.500 - 750) sub-periods," Record states. Excavated" artifacts recovered are typical of Native American sites in the Glades region," Record states. These artifacts have a direct historical connection with the Tequesta Indians.

A public outcry commenced when the Miami Herald reported in early 1999, "Archaeologists find ancient cemetery, near a mysterious stone circle," Historic Record states. This site record has a total of 567 pages, so if anyone wants to read the record, call Tallahassee or go to your county office. The Miami Circle record includes 24 newspaper articles and letters that follows the events from 1998 to 2002.

The first letter, February 14, 1999, is from Becky Matkov, Executive Director, Dade Heritage Trust, to George Percy, Florida Department of State, Historic Preservation Division, Tallahassee. "The request was for the State of Florida to assume jurisdiction over the Brickell Pointe development property in Miami, 401 Brickell Avenue, at the mouth of the Miami River. Under Florida Statue 872.05(5), "Discovery of an Unmarked Human Burial During an Archaeological Excavation," Florida law defines "unmarked human burial" as any human skeletal remains or associated burial artifacts or any location, including any burial mound or earthen or shell monument, where human skeletal remains or associated burial artifacts are DISCOVERED or BELIEVED to exist on the basis of archaeological or historical evidence," Record states.

An emergency situation is occurring over the mysterious circle cut into stone. The developer has city permits to build his $126 million project and a backhoe sits at the back chain-link fence. Governor Jeb Bush's office reported receiving 317 phone calls and 367 emails to stop the project. "Leading Miami-Dade County Preservationists argue, the state has not gone far enough to impose its own laws against the developer," Record states. On February 15, 1999 a petition circulated demanding government agencies block the construction." April 12, 1999, an evidentiary hearing for Miami-Dade County's attempt to take the circle site under eminent domain. The suit alleges the city failed to follow its own historic preservation ordinances when issuing building permits to developer Michael Baumann," Record states. This is the first eminent domain case ever undertaken in the state of Florida to protect an archaeological site. Baumann would be compensated for the loss of the property.

How much is the 2.2 acre parcel worth? H. Cantrell of Jacksonville appraised the property's worth at $38 million. B. Diskin of Tallahassee said the worth was $42 million. Both estimates are not shockers, Baumann hired them. Two county appraiser, B. Gallaher placed the value at $17 million, and the second appraiser, L Johnson, fair market value was lower, at $15 million. Gallaher said, the project should be divided into three components: Planning, Construction and Marketing. Baumann paid $8 million for the land in 1998. At the November 30, 2000 deadline, the county assembled $26.7 million from three sources to purchase the parcel. " State of Florida took title, while the county as the lessee of the land, is required to provide a management plan to the state within one year," Record states.

"A special committee set up to safeguard the Miami Circle-- has endorsed a plan to protect the site from the elements while making the site available to the public," Record states. May 15, 2002, "United States Senator Bob Graham filed a bill calling for the Department of the Interior to study whether the Circle should become part of the National Park system," Record states. Miami Circle Planning Group approved a proposal to erect a 60-foot tall thatched roof build over the circle with a contoured path. M. Spring, Director of Miami-Dade County's Cultural Affairs, called this an interim project to protect the circle from rain and erosion, but allows the public to view area's historical site, while waiting to hear from National Park Service. Years later, the National Park Service reviewed the Miami Circle but rejected the idea of adding the 2.2 acre Circle to the Park System.

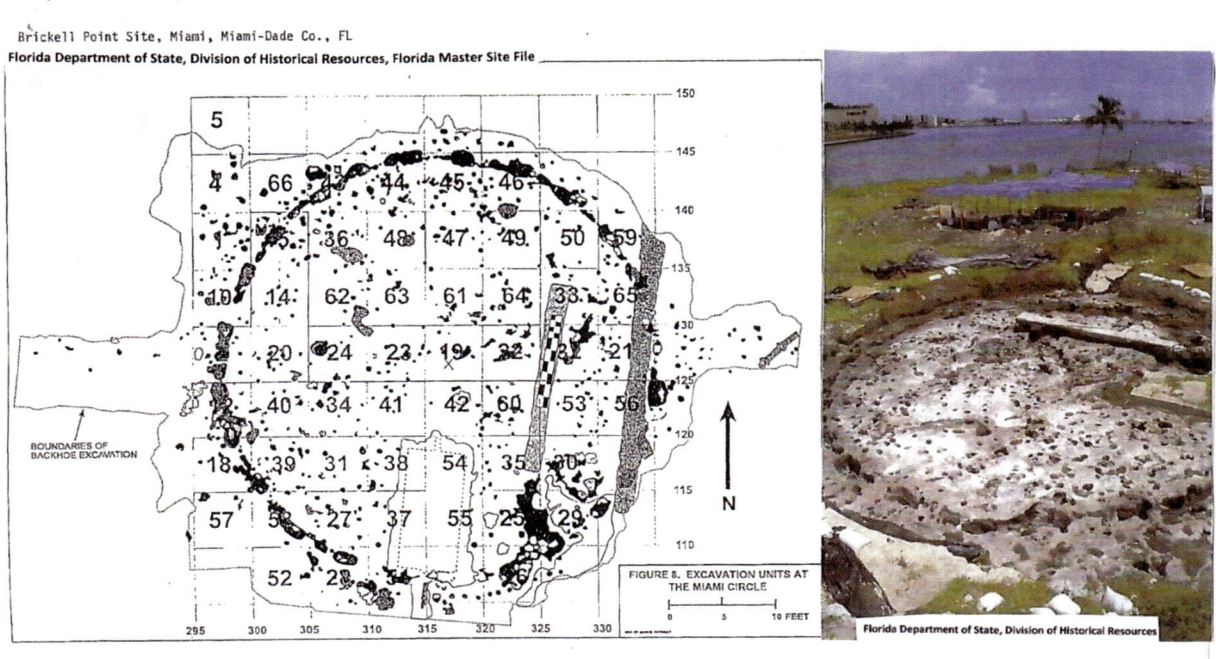

MUD LAKE CANAL

Flamingo, Florida
MONROE COUNTY

NATIONAL LANDMARK 2006

The owner of this site is the Everglades National Park, the National Park Service, the Federal Government. Unlike other canals, Mud Lake is not damaged by agricultural, sand mining, or development and is protected in the park setting.

The size of Mud Lake is 46.7 acres. The location is South Western Florida near the coastal waters of Gulf of Mexico or the southern tip of the mainland continental United States, "at the edge of the world," Record states. Canal stretches 3.9 miles in length across the marsh lands. Mud Lake Canal is significantly designed for the purpose of travel of people between Miami River/Biscayne Bay, upper Florida Keys and the Ten Thousand Islands.

Southern Florida Sites Associated with the Tequesta and their Ancestors Study and the "long distance canoe canals associated with the Tequesta people in the Everglades of southern Florida," Record states. (The Tequesta Native tribe name was the focus in the Miami Circle, the preceding chapter.) A long-distance canoe canal involves planning and constructing details, an understanding of local topographic (surface features) and hydrologic (water cycle) conditions to avoid saltwater intrusion. Hurricane damage has deposited marl from the canals.

Florida Bay covered parts of the canal banks, "which probably has aided in preserving deposits that can be radiocarbon dated," Record states.

"Mud Lake Canal was dug by American Indians and may have been designed to provide safe passage, easy access to aquatic resources, and courses for exchange, like other long distance canoe canals in Florida, "Record states. The mastery of the Tequesta Indians illustrates major aptitude and skills.

A historical fiction book, *A Land Remembered,* nominated for a Pulitzer Prize, was written about this time period about Tequesta natives. The book's Indian legends and cultural heritage clarifies how they survive in the Cypress Swamp. Author Patrick D. Smith referred to the natives as Seminoles, which was incorrect. Seminoles were in, Northern Panhandle part of the state. Even University of Miami Professor Tebeau, *History of Florida,* refers to many native groups as Seminoles, so the writers guess is Seminoles has become a generic term.

Everglades Park is the largest wilderness area east of the Mississippi, so consider the wildlife you can see for the first time. You can check in at Flamingo Visitor Center for canoeing directions and a weather report before your canoe trip,that starts at Coot Bay Pond. You cross Buttonwood Canal, travel along the shore line to connect to the celebrated Mud Lake Canal, where the native

Tequesta Tribe lived and dug the canal systems.

Florida Department of State, Division of Historical Resources, Florida Master Site File

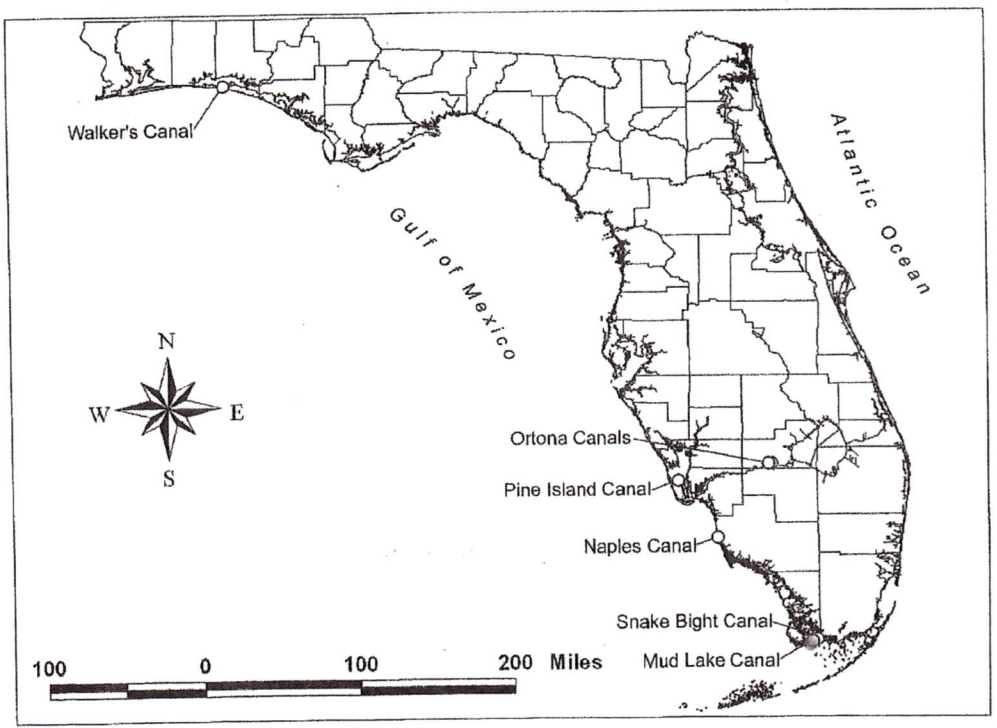

Figure 9. Map showing Florida canoe canals.

Florida Department of State, Division of Historical Resources, Florida Master Site File

Betty Grable Poster

Norman Film Manufacturing Company

6337 Arlington Road
Jacksonville, Florida

National Landmark 2016

Are you acquainted with the silent film industry that flourished in Jacksonville in 1908? Jacksonville was widely known as the Winter Film Capital. Norman Studios is Jacksonville's only remaining silent film studio, with a unique contribution to African-American Cinema.

Jacksonville's warm weather and exotic plantation homes with hanging moss made the winter resort a popular choice for many film studios. Cheaper labor costs in Jacksonville for "extras" and "mob scenes" made the southern city very desirable compared to New York City. Kalem Studios opened its doors in 1908, producing more than 30 silent films in Jacksonville. Metro Pictures, later MGM, first created films in 1915 in this Florida city. Nevertheless, Southern California's pleasant climate and open spaces beckoned. Large studios headed west in the late teens.

Richard Norman "earned a living by producing small comedies for Midwestern audiences starring with their own local talent," states the historic record. Caucasian Florida native Richard Norman, "was a traveling filmmaker for a decade before returning home" to Jacksonville. He was born in Middleburg, Florida in 1891, attended college in Tampa, majoring in chemistry and motion pictures.

In 1916 his first full-length movie release, "The Green-Eyed Monster", found a favorable outcome with an all-black cast. Norman Films, Lincoln Motion Picture Company and Oscar Micheaux produced "race" movies presenting black actors in a positive roles. Norman's next release, in 1921, "The Bull Dogger" a western shot in

Oklahoma giving audiences an opportunity to see black cowboys in action."

Norman wrote and produced his next action silent film at the Arlington Studio, "The Flying Ace" in 1926, starring Bessie Coleman. The first black women licensed pilot who was famous for her "heart thrilling stunts," and who "died in a fiery crash over Jacksonville." (A rare copy of the "The Flying Ace" resides at the Library of Congress in Washington, D.C.)

Norman Studio's success continued with production of his silent race films from 1920 to 1928. In this time frame Norman Studios produced eight films and comedy shorts. They were: "The Love Bug" "The Green-Eyed Monster ," "The Crimson Skull," "The Bull-Dogger," "Regeneration", " A Debtor to the Law," "The Flying Ace," and "The Black Gold." "He stopped making race films in the late 1920s," the record states.

The Arlington Road two-story Frame Vernacular property with NORMAN LABORATORIES, written across the top was actually constructed as a "cigar factory in 1913 by R.K. Shaw and H. M Lott" from Quincy, Florida. Their factory plan failed.

By 1915 the site was made available to Eagle Film City. On the 1.65 acre site, Eagle Film City improved the front two-story structure by converting the main office into a property room, developing and drying rooms, storage vault and a projection room. A large garage (Building #4) was constructed," in addition to lounging pavilions, dressing rooms, artist's quarters, director's bungalows, stages, and an outdoor swimming pool (used for filming ocean and river scenes)." For self-sufficiency, "the Eagle Film City constructed its own electric and water plant." In January 1916 the "Florida Times Union" reported Eagle Film spent "$48,000 to locate a plant and studio." The Eagle Film Company produced a series of short comedies that met with limited success. Their "national leasing agency, Unity Sales

Corporation, went out of business" and in the "spring of 1917, Eagle Film City went bankrupt."

Arlington Road "facility sat abandoned until it was purchased in 1922 at a bargain price by film producer, director, and writer Richard Norman" the record states. Competition for a fully-equipped studio was non-existent because all the other studios moved to California. Norman controlled the best studio in the city by going against the trend and relocating back to Jacksonville. Norman produced at this location until the late 1920's.

Visionary Norman invested his savings into his new patented invention of a synchronization device by joining picture and voice together. He sold the devices to theater owners for $6,000 each. He expected big profits until Western Electric produced a competitive apparatus. However, Richard Norman "is credited as being one of the first to synchronize sound and motion on the theater screen." He shifted to making "industrial films for commercial enterprises such as the Pure Oil Company." Also Norman shifted into film distribution with his many industry contacts and operated a movie theater. He retired in 1952.

Norman's wife Gloria introduced a Dance School in 1935, using the second floor of the main building, # 1, that served as the headquarters. The successful dance school had 200 students at one time. Gloria gave instruction in ballet, tap, acrobatic and ball room dancing until 1975. Promptly, "Gloria

Norman put the property up for sale" the historic record stated.

The open, expansive, attractive property with five Frame Vernacular structures includes much green space between the buildings. The main "Headquarters" front structure faces Arlington Road, where the street was "widened to include much of the property's front right of way." The two-story structure in height with a hipped roof, overhanging eaves, exposed rafters, holds a small brick chimney on the west slope of the roof. Building one, Headquarters, holds a centrally-placed double front entrance topped by a one-light transom window. Building # two was designed to house the electric generator with the control panel that powered the studio. Building three has the same structure qualities as the rest of the complex. This building served as the dressing room and prop house for the studio. Building four served as a garage and storage facility and housed a second power generator, powering the water tower. The water tower was demolished in 1970s but the foundation is still visible, as reported in the Historic Record. Building five served as a residence for visiting actors and later as the Gloria Norman School of Dance. On the front grounds closer to Arlington Road of Building five, was the in ground pool used for filming water scenes but the pool has been filled in. Lot five and building, has been sold to Circle of Faith Ministries and re-purposed as a church.

Presently the property, .82 acreage, is owned by the City of Jacksonville, Real Estate Division. In 2011 "Jacksonville prepares to transfer the historic film studio to the Federal Park System," the historic record states. In 2003, former Governor Jeb Bush announced the creation of the UNCF/Richard E. Norman Scholarships, available at Florida's colleges and universities with film programs.

Movie Safe

This property is the "best preserved studio complexes from the silent film era in the country," states the historic record and is Jacksonville's only surviving silent film studio.

Historic marker at Okeechobee Battlefield

OKEECHOBEE BATTLEFIELD

OKEECHOBEE COUNTY

This last venue was an attempt of the United States Army to remove American Indians from Florida. The Battle's site boundary has always been in question. The boundary resolve came 169 years later with the purchase of acreage by the State of Florida.

Spain ceded Florida to the United States in 1821. Osceola died in prison in Fort Moutrie, Charleston, South Carolina in January 30, 1838. The anticipated loss pulled the other chiefs-- Wildcat, Apeika, Alligator, Coacoochee, and Halleck Tustenuggee together to fight expulsion from Florida. The action was Emigrate or Fight!

The largest and bloodiest battle of the Third Seminole War was fought on Christmas Day 1837. The white man's difficulty was a lack of knowledge of Florida's interior. The large interior lake, Lake Okeechobee, was omitted from the famous 1837 map. A call went out for volunteers. Troops came from Missouri and Pennsylvania and joined General Jesup. By October 1, Jesup had 9000 troops. "Delays kept the army out of action until December," Historic Record states. Colonel Zackary Taylor, with 600 Missouri Volunteers, departed on transport ships to Florida, along with 800 regulars.

On Christmas Day, Taylor found 400 Indians waiting to attack. The Indian position was carefully chosen on a sand ridge, separated from the pineland and ¾ mile from the impassable swamp. The scrub grass was cut down for 20 yards for a clear firing field. Indians watched the Army's progress from the cypress trees. Trees were notched to support the Indians guns. "The ridge formed an escape route to the east and west," Record States. Chief Alligator later said there were 380 warriors. Taylor's command consisted of 803 men but he used only 369 men in the assault. "The Army found crossing the swamp difficult. The troops waded through three feet of water, and saw grass cut their skin, giving many eye injuries from the sharp grass blades," Record states. Taylor's men charged after crossing the swamp directly at the enemy. The battle-line advanced and the soldiers fired from behind the trees. "A hideous yell" from the Indians and the fire volley continued for hours. "The Seminoles lost eleven killed and fourteen wounded and killed twenty-six whites and wounded 112 in a fight that lasted from about a half hour past noon to three o'clock," Dr. Tebeau stated. "The war continued on with hit-and-run attacks for another five years, but the defeat of the Native Americans at this Battle of Okeechobee, marked the turning point in the struggle, as they never again engaged in a pitched battle," Record states. Both sides claimed victory. Taylor, "Old Rough and Ready," was assigned to the First Department of the Army Headquarters in Louisiana. His victories during the Mexican War, caused the Whig party to nominate him for President.

Willard Steele's book, *The Battle of Okeechobee,* describes unexpected war details. Steele's distinctive description of the Indian Chiefs continues. Chief Alligator "the most shrewd, crafty, politic, and intelligent chief of the Seminole nation," Record states. He spoke English and associated with the settlers on friendly terms. Alligator was best known as a tactician, and his "great knowledge of the country made him a dangerous enemy on the battlefield." Alligator was chosen "as a delegate to go west to investigate the reservation land, as a prerequisite to the removal of Indians. The delegation strongly expressed dissatisfaction with Arkansas," Record states. The Government sent the delegation there in the dead of winter, which is no future for the Florida Indians. The chiefs made their decision, "not to leave the country, but to fight for it," Record states. "Chief Coacoochee, Wildcat who had escaped from the fort at St. Augustine only the previous month, and was the influential single event that led to the Battle of Okeechobee," Dr. Tebeau states.

After the war, Chief Alligator "escaped with his people, but the offensive movement of the Army caused him to surrender in April 1838. He was removed to Arkansas in 1839, returned to Florida to help the Army negotiate with different bands—to be moved back to Arkansas," Record states. Wildcat was sent to Arkansas, "twice (1844, 1850), led groups of Seminoles off the reservation. Wildcat's group moved to Mexico and he obtained land from that government in exchange for fighting against the Comanche. Wildcat died in Mexico in

1857," Record States. Apeika, (Sam Jones), Seminoles Spiritual Leader, who was between 70 and 90 years of age, eluded the Army by moving to Pine Island. His time was spent attempting to maintain peace between the Seminoles and the Army. Halleck Tushenuggee eluded capture until April 1841, sent to Arkansas and died on the reservation.

During the 1961 Landmark application process, the site's boundaries were not clearly defined. "The National Park Service has been working to establish boundaries for all National Historic Landmarks for which no specific boundary was identified at the time of application," Record states. First, goal is to locate the battlefield, second to preserve some portion of the battlefield, third, to assist the State and "Okeechobee community commemorate the 150th Anniversary of the battle." State designation encompassed 140 acres, while National Landmark designation encompassed over 1300 acres. Where is the battlefield located?

An archaeological firm was hired to investigate activity areas and graves sites locations. Geosphere Inc, was hired for remote sensing testing and 357 shovel tests performed, placing them at 20 foot intervals in all directions of the site. In the search for the graves, the center of Taylor Camp site and to the north, an additional 47 potholes were dug. The total of potholes was 654 at a depth of three feet in the grave search. The graves were located. A second interment relocated the soldier's remains to the National Cemetery in St. Augustine, in the same manner as the soldiers from the Dade Battlefield in 1842.

"The National Trust for Historic Preservation joined the effort in 2000 by listing the battlefield, as one of the country's 11 most endangered historic sites, record states. The locals did not know the battlefield existed, as it was not even mentioned in school. A roadside historic marker next to a chicken restaurant suggests the battlefield site was at this spot but the marker was moved. Preservations were afraid rapid growth in the city of Okeechobee would turn the site into a subdivision or shopping area.

Miami Herald article was titled "Old Battlefield just fading away," where significant events occurred during the Second Seminole War. The +211 acres now consists of improved pasture and freshwater marsh, provides the backdrop for reenactment of the battle. The cultural significance is a smaller part of a larger battlefield site. Seminoles avoided capture and removal from Florida but found sanctuary in the Everglades and never surrendered. "The Seminole Tribe and others have been fighting to preserve the historic site. In 2006, Governor Jeb Bush and the Florida Cabinet agreed to spend $3.2 million to purchase 145.5 acres, where Seminole, Miccosukee Indians and escaped black slaves fought hand-to-hand with the U.S. Army on Christmas Day 1837," Record states.

For contact information, Okeechobee Battlefield Historic State Park, the number is 863-462-5360.

PELICAN ISLAND NATIONAL WILDLIFE REFUGE

South of Sebastian
Indian River County

National Landmark 1963

Floridians honor the late President Theodore Roosevelt, who in 1903 established by Executive Order the first sanctuary for the protection of wildlife. The Rookery forms a nesting home for brown pelicans, egrets, herons, ibis, and spoonbills for a total of 16 species of water birds. Before Pelican Island is now about a third of its original size setting in the middle of mild flowing Indian River Lagoon.

By the late 19th Century, the fashion industry requested bird feathers that resulted in the slaughter of appealing herons, egrets, spoonbills and pelicans. "In 1858 Dr. Henry Bryant witnessed the slaughter of sixty spoonbills a day on Pelican Island." The plume hunters and egg collectors are restricted by federal law, Lacey Act passed in 1904. The Florida Audubon

Society and the American Ornithologists' Union also had a state law passed to protect non-game birds. A fellow conservationist convinced President Theodore Roosevelt to protect Pelican Island. Paul Kroegel was hired as the first federal wildlife warden in April 1903. The island's size was approximately five-acres when Warden Kroegel's service commenced.

Another threat emerged from trade fisherman in the spring of 1918. Fisherman believed the pelicans were eating their game fish. Over 400 defenseless pelican chicks were clubbed to death on Pelican Island. Audubon Society members proved to the fisherman that the pelican's diet consisted of unimportant baitfish. Many species of birds have returned to the island, to their special nesting home of more than a hundred years.

In the 1960's a new threat unfolded, when attempts to sell surrounding wetland islands to developers arose. Local citizens groups teamed with the Audubon Society to stop the sale of these wetlands. Audubon Society advanced the issue to the State of Florida "to include 422 acres of mangrove islands as part of the refuge. In 1968, the State of Florida agreed to expand the lease with the refuge to include 4,760 acres of mangrove islands and submerged lands."

Erosion from freezes, storms and excess bird dropping continue to kill off the mangroves. Boat waves action eat away at mangrove roots and marsh grasses, causing more erosion. "From 1970 to 2000, the island lost 55 percent of its size to erosion," say fish and wildlife officials.

In February 2001, "the federal government dumped 250 tons of oyster shells from a Black Hawk Helicopter to build a protective barrier between the island and the waves." Additional plans include placing 3,000 cubic yards of sand on the island, to build a sandbar to slow boat wakes.

Pelican Island is closed to the public; nevertheless charters from Sebastian take visitors within a few hundred yards of the island to view the 16 species of birds on the island. In 2003 a 50-foot Observation Tower was constructed for viewing, along with a 500 foot wooden broad walk.

For additional information contact a ranger at 772-562-3909, Ext. 258, also 888-404-3922 or visit the Web site, pelicanisland.fws.gov.

*Note the appendix references and selected reading references.

PENSACOLA NAVAL AIR STATION HISTORIC DISTRICT

Pensacola, Florida
Escambia County
National Landmark 1976

As our team crossed over the Pensacola Bay Bridge, the Blue Angels soared above in their classic Diamond Formation, passing up into the white clouds. What a welcome seeing the Blue Angels in practice. Blue Angels are the Navy's precision flying team. Blue Angels flight demonstrations are in their 72nd year of performing throughout the United States. Aerial displays began in 1946, and now perform routinely 70 shows at 34 locations each year in the United States. Shows are tailored to local weather conditions from March until November. Since 1946, an estimated 260 million spectators took pleasure in their flying aerobatic extravaganza.

The modern Pensacola Naval Air Station Historic District encompasses 8,622 acres of enormous historic significance. In these boundaries another National Landmark Fort San Carlos De Barrances is sited. The site will be illustrated in its own chapter.

The National Historic Landmark data base affirms in their statement of significance as: Naval Air Station was established in January 1914 as the United States First Permanent Naval Air Station, First Navy Pilot Training Center, and First U.S. Naval Installation to send pilots into combat. "Secretary of the Navy, Josephus Daniels ordered the creation of a permanent naval air station, where the climate favored year-round flying."

Building 45 # Naval Air Station Headquarters

Historic Pensacola began when Andrew Jackson accepts from Spain the transfer of

Florida to the United States in 1821. Surrounded by large timber reserves, a shipbuilding facility was established near the Pensacola harbor, because the Florida coastline needed substantial protection. In March 1824, "Congress approved the establishment of a naval base at

Pensacola." Secretary of the Navy Samuel Southard choose a site selection committee. The group chose a location south in Escambia County and near the mouth of Pensacola Bay. Without a master plan, work proceeded slowly for shipbuilding, repair and Navy Base establishment.

In the time span of 15 years (1829-1844) prior to the Mexican War, rapid development of their defenses occurred.

The new forts erected were Fort Pickens on Santa Rosa Island, Fort McRee on Peridido Key, and Fort Redoubt west of the yard. Fort Barrancas was strengthened with brick and earthwork, assuming an invasion from Mexico.

The Mexican War occurred from 1846 to 1848, and resulted in the United States gaining 525,000 square miles of new territory. The Mexican War trained many officers,1- Ulysses S. Grant, 2- Robert E. Lee, 3-Stonewall Jackson, 4- Jefferson Davis for the approaching Civil War.

The Navy Yard moved forward between 1855 and 1859, by erecting 60 structures for yard work and living quarters. "The Civil War (1861-65) interrupted this progress." Florida seceded early from the union in 1861. Union forces held Fort Pickens on Santa Rosa Island, controlling the month of Pensacola Bay that could be easily reinforced with supplies from this vantage point. Confederate forces occupied Forts Barrancas and McRee with support from 500 Alabama troops, and held the valuable navy yard.

Cannon fire was exchanged across Pensacola Bay. February 1862, Confederates removed all useful machinery, cannons, guns, large and small, from the navy yard, and its commissary stores. On May 7 they burned the remains, marine hospital, barracks and two small steamers and evacuated north to strengthen other Civil War field armies. Union forces re-occupied the yard, cleared away fire rubble and erected new structures. *A History of Florida,* Professor Tebeau reports," Pensacola remained a ghost town."

Congress appropriated funding to rebuild the Navy Yard completing the task: dock basin gates, houses, shops, modern power plant, new wharf, wireless stations and 10,000 ton floating dry dock. In 1898 the Spanish-American War lasted from April to August and sparked a revival of activity at the Navy Yard.

The Panama Canal construction kept interest high at the historic facility. In 1906 a killer hurricane "lashed the area and destroyed or damaged nearly every major yard structure." For 4 years Washington navy officials debated the future of the Navy Yard. Five other bases fulfilled the Navy's needs and in 1911 the Federal Government closed the Pensacola Navy Yard.

The new Secretary of the Navy, Josephus Daniels, appointed a board to "prepare a comprehensive plan for the organization of Naval Aeronautic Service." December 1913 Daniels ordered all aviation personnel and equipment to Pensacola. In 1914 the first United States Naval Air Station (NAS) was established at Pensacola. "Aviation, then in its infancy, was important to Florida." Pensacola's NAS entire command consisted of seven seaplanes, six qualified pilots, 23 enlisted men, spare plane parts, and canvas hangers. The pilots trained tough and had many accomplishments. A short time later, eight weeks, Pensacola NAS became the "first American military branch to send pilots and planes into combat."

Flights over enemy lines proved a great assistance to military operations. "Commander H.C. Mustin made the first successful catapult launching from a ship, by flying off the stern of the U.S. North Carolina in Pensacola Bay." New altitude records of 16,000 feet were set. NAS's duties included," training personnel, maintaining and repairing school aircraft, testing new planes, aircraft body, engine and instrument design, constructing new kinds of aircrafts, collecting performance data from experimental and training flights" historical record states.

When the United States entered World War I in 1917, "NAS had 38 naval aviators, 163 enlisted men in training and 54 airplanes." Two years later "the air station had 438 officers and 5,538 enlisted men with 1,000 trained aviators". At the war's end "seaplanes, dirigibles, kite balloons and aerial photography expanded to meet war demand." The Navy Department ordered great expansion at NAS "to construct an auxiliary field, five miles northwest and named after 23rd flight student, Commander W.A. Corry who served with distinction in World War I." The 530 acre Corry Field was dedicated on November 1, 1928, as an auxiliary field base.

World War II witnessed the fall of France in 1939. The Japanese attack occurred on Pearl Harbor December 7, 1941. "President F.D. Roosevelt called for 126,000 planes." Pensacola NAS base commander, Captain A.C. Read, "expanded training to 1,100 cadets a month, 11 times the amount trained annually in the 1920s." Three more auxiliary fields, Bronson, Barin, and Whiting, all named for early naval aviators, needed to produce the quota of men for the war emergency. Pensacola NAS adjusted its "training schedule to accommodate 2,300 students per month, an increase of 300 percent" and produced 20,000 pilots. "The total number of enemy aircraft destroyed by the U.S Navy and Marine Corps was 15,401." They sank 63 German submarines and 161 Japanese warships. "Then Senator O. Brewster's stated: the growth of naval aviation during World War II is one of the wonders of the modern world." record states. Japanese surrendered in August 1945 and the war ended. The formal Peace Treaty was signed in April 28, 1952.

June 25, 1950, North Korea invaded South Korea. President Truman ordered U.S. air and naval forces to defend South Korea on June 27, 1950. New on the NAS training syllabus were jet planes, despite the fact that propeller planes proved their importance in other wars. The NAS center revised its training techniques from propeller planes to jets engines, and "produced 6,000 aviators from 1950 to 1953."

Pensacola NAS tradition of leadership continued into the Vietnam War, (1965 -

1973). "Pilot training was as low as 1,413 (1962) and as high as 2,552 (1968)." Three American Presidents, Kennedy, Johnson and Nixon committed aid, support and combat forces to the Vietnam conflict to prevent the country from falling to communism domination. In November 1967, President Johnson increased combat troops upward to an estimated 500,000. U.S. and South Vietnamese forces relied on dependable air superiority. Large anti-war protects broke out in Washington D.C. Nixon won the presidency in 1969.

A gradual withdrawal of U.S forces began to end American involvement and let the South Vietnamese fight for themselves. Paris Peace Accord was signed by all parties in January 1973 but the fighting continued. Saigon was captured by the North and the two were reunified in 1975.

"Pensacola Naval Air Station Historic District includes 55 designated historic structures." The three periods of construction are: (1-)1865 to 1899, "rebuilt after the destruction by Confederate-set fires during the Civil War; (2-)1906 to 1908, rebuilt after the devastating hurricane damage of 1906; and (3-)1916 to 1918, when the first air station structures, including hangers, were erected." The significant seaplane metal hangers are buildings #71, 72, 73, 74, 75, and 76. Hurricane Ivan in 2004 severely damaged hangers #71, 72, 76 and they were demolished.

Other significant structure #16, 120 Center Avenue, and constructed in 1854, survived the Civil War, defined in 1976

#16 Legal Services

historic record, as Armory Chapel. The distinctive, one-of-kind octagonal, two-story, salmon-colored brick, double–tiered, is utilized now as the Region Legal Service Office.

Commanding Officer's Quarters, Building Q-1, referred to today Quarters A. Architectural style is Italianate, three story of tan brick with a white-trim, two-tiered screened veranda, built in 1874.

Behind this structure are stables #19 and #28 again tan brick, build in 1874. Power Plant #47A, erected in 1907, striking red brick, semicircular fanlight windows, in molded-brick arch with highly ornate cornices decorate the upper walls. This beautiful structure is on the list of expendable buildings but now serves as a repair shop.

Headquarters #45, is located at the center of the Historic District and near the water front across South Avenue. Built in 1907, the three story red brick structure serves as Naval Air Station headquarters today. "Many striking features are an exposed granite-block foundation, triple first-story windows set under semicircular fanlights," on page one.   Structure was converted from industrial use.

National Naval Aviation Museum is one of the most-visited museums in Florida. The museum's mission," is to select, collect, preserve and display historic artifacts." The main collection includes aircraft, flight simulators, assorted uniforms, fight gear, weaponry, medals, and decorations. "The museum also received the prestigious American Association of Museums accreditation in 2002." Admission is free and the museum is open daily from 9 a.m. to 5:00 p.m., call 800-327-5002.

Note the Appendix reference records and Selected Reading for all references.

PLAZA FERDINAND VII

Pensacola, Florida

Escambia County

National Landmark 1960

The highest significant landmark site in the State of Florida is Plaza Ferdinand VII. The formal transfer of Florida from Spain to the United States officially established the Florida Territory.

The Rule of Spain ended with the Adams-Onis Treaty of July 22, 1819. Spain agreed to surrender Florida to United States in exchange for claims against the Spanish government for five million dollars. Spain finally ratified the treaty on February 22, 1821.

General Andrew Jackson received a commission as governor on March 12, 1821. His responsibility was to establish territorial government and to receive and occupy the ceded lands of East and West Florida.

General Jackson "appointed Colonel Robert Butler, as his deputy, to accept the transfer of East Florida" occurring in St. Augustine. The transfer of East Florida was achieved first on July 10. Both Jackson and Butler encountered delaying tactics from the Spanish governors. A third transfer ceremony occurred at Fort St. Marks. Spanish troops were delayed on their final sail out because of unfavorable winds, but they arrived in Pensacola on July 19, 1821.

The final transfer ceremony happened in Pensacola, July 17, 1821. At 10 a.m. Governor Jackson rode to the Government House (now City Hall) met with Spanish

Governor Callava and walked together to the plaza. The Fourth Infantry band played "The Star-Spangled Banner," the Spanish flag was lowered to half-staff and the American flag was raised to the same level. In Pensacola Bay the **USS Hornet** fired a 21-gun salute, the Spanish flag was lowered and the American flag was raised to full staff. Of the three transfer ceremonies, Pensacola was the most significant one, due to the fact the territorial Governor participated and proclaimed the transfer complete. The ceremony marked the first occasion when the "Star-Spangled Banner" played at a public function in Florida.

The historic Plaza built by the British around 1775 that is bounded by Government, Jefferson, Zaragoza and Palafox Streets. The Spanish King in 1808 gave his name to the square but the British changed the name to "Square of the Constitution"; later the Spanish reversed the name.

Livestock roamed in the plaza until 1889 when citizens requested landscaping and better style. "The first ornamental iron water fountain was erected –and was completely electrified with incandescent lights." The 1909 fountain was restored and reinstalled in 1974.

W.D. Chipley Monument anchored the plaza for bringing the L & N Railroad to Pensacola. In 1935 the Andrew Jackson Monument stationed on granite completed the plaza among the many trees honoring leading Pensacola citizens.

Andrew Jackson was elected President of the United States in 1828. Jackson's victory against the British in the War of 1812, made him a national hero. His presidency might be best known for the "Indian Removal Act." Many Native American tribes were told to relocate to the West, some tribes did so willingly while others resisted. The "Resistance" was at the heart of Florida's, bitter and costly Seminole wars.

*Note the appendix references and selected reading references.

PONCE de LEON INLET LIGHT STATION

4931 South Peninsula Drive
Ponce Inlet
Volusia County
National Landmark 1998

You can step back in time and experience what it was like living at this isolated location in the late 1800s. Shipwrecks along the east coast of Florida between St. Augustine and Cape Canaveral were increasing. The light station is significant for its association with Federal efforts to provide a unified system of navigational aids to insure safe maritime transportation. The 175-foot tall Ponce de Leon is the second tallest light house on the Eastern Seaboard, only the 191-footer at Cape Hatteras, North Carolina, is taller.

The first lighthouse built at Mosquito Inlet in 1835 was wooden construction and suffered due to coastal storms. Unrest in the form of the Second Seminole War caused violence to increase in the area that made repair of the damaged lighthouse impossible. In 1887 the structure finally collapsed. The Federal Government purchased the present 40 acre site and construction began in 1887 on the new light house.

Brick was used for construction with granite embellishments. On the North side of the stepped entrance, nine granite steps at the base were formed entirely of granite, and the doorway reflects a classic order of simple angular pediment with the frieze omitted to avoid undue heaviness. On the south side of the conical tower, four windows conform to the shape of the arch above. The tower tapers from a 32-foot diameter base to a 12-foot diameter top. The brick walls are eight feet thick at the

base and two feet thick at the top. The tower first lighted the night on January 6, 1888.

The light came from burning oil in lamps. Can you imagine carrying the oil supply up the tower's 213 steps each day? The exterior tower glass had to be cleaned often so the light beam could reflect out, 20 miles to the sea. These were some of the job responsibilities of the keepers.

"The station was converted to electricity in 1920s, and, at the same time, the name Mosquito Inlet was changed to Ponce de Leon Inlet," historic record states. After the conversion to electricity, the need for keepers was abolished. The first order fixed lens was removed and replaced with a third order revolving (flashing) Fresnel lens, which is on displace in the museum now. The new lens remained operational in the tower until March 1970. When the light station tower was decommissioned in flavor of a new light across the inlet at the Coast Guard Station" report confirms. With the construction of a new high-rise beach condominium that obscured the light at the Coast Guard Station, the Coast Guard reactivated the Ponce de Leon Inlet Lighthouse in December 1982. "Lightning destroyed the FA251-AC rotating light in 1996 and it was replaced by a VBR-25 Marine Rotating Beacon," landmark record stated.

The park, lighthouse, out buildings fell into a state of neglect and vandalism occurred. Preliminary park restoration began soon after Town of Ponce de Inlet was created in 1963. The keeper's residence turned into town meeting halls. Restoration is directed by the Ponce de Leon Inlet Preservation Association.

Principal Keeper's, First Assistant Keeper's and Second Assistant Keeper's Dwellings were all built in 1887 of brick construction, 1 story structures with fireplaces, assigned square footage of 680, with front and back

porches. Bathrooms were added in 1921 along with other upgrades. All keeper's houses roofs are replaced. All keeper cottages are decorated in period styles and used for museum display purposes today.

The 1887 Oil house made of brick with a hipped roof and "four cross shaped ventilation holes formed into the brick walls. The door was originally copper sheeted for fire protection" but replaced now with a heavy wooden door, states the landmark record. "Two large iron storage tanks located in the oil house date back to 1927." The house suffered a fire in the 1970s which destroyed the copper roof and much of the interior. Total restoration cost was $30,000 in 1989.

Three brick wood sheds/privies were constructed about 1887 and all are located near the keeper's houses. "In 1933 the wood shed behind the first assistant keeper's dwelling was turned into a generator building and a radio room was added to the north side in 1943." Today, the structure is now the home of the video theatre.

The frame pump house with tin roof replaced the well and windmill. "The eight-foot Samson windmill was disassembled about 1914 and the water tower existed to about 1952." Wharf deteriorated and washed away. Keeper's garage was torn down in 1972. By 1914 two boat houses existed, one on shore, the other on the dock, both are gone. The Main Entrance Building and Gift Shop, 2 ½ story, build in 1992 contains offices, restrooms and a gift shop. Gift shop features a wide assortments of maritime gifts.

In the Ponce de Leon Light Station Village, in 1995 new construction added the Lens Exhibit Building or museum. Exhibits explain the history and technology of lighthouse illumination and "clamshell" Fresnel lens restoration. The lighthouse original first order Fresnel lens from 1887 to 1933 is on display, with other significant navigational aids.

"Ponce de Leon is one of the nation's best preserved complete light stations, retaining its tower, all three of its keepers dwelling, oil house, and combination woodshed/privies" landmark record states.

The lighthouse area as it appears today is surrounded by a white picket fence. The site is a favorite for tourists, with a white sandy beach around the corner. Should you want more information, call 386-761-1821. Credit and thank you is given to the Ponce De Inlet Lighthouse Preservation Association, Inc. for their diagram.

RAWLINGS, MARJORIE KINNAN, HISTORIC STATE PARK
National Landmark 2006

18700 South Cr 325
Cross Creek, Florida
Alachua County

Marjorie Kinnan Rawlings won the Pulitzer Prize in 1939 for *The Yearling*. She is among many female authors who have gone before her as Pulitzer Prize Winners: Margaret Mitchell for *Gone with the Wind* in 1937, Pearl S. Buck for *The Good Earth* in 1932, Margaret A. Barnes for *Years of Grace* in 1931, Julia M Peterkin for *Scarlet Sister Mary* in 1929, Edna Ferber for *So Big* in 1925, Margaret Wilson for *The Able McLaughlins* in 1924, Willa Cather for *One of Ours* in 1923, Edith Wharton for *Age of Innocence* in 1921. Decades passed before another female won. Harper Lee won for *To Kill a Mockingbird* in 1961. Pulitzer Prize honors outstanding achievements in journalism, literature, music and the arts.

Marjorie Kinnan was born in Washington, D.C. in 1896, in the Brookland neighborhood, to an upper middle class family. Her father was an attorney for the US Patent Office. Her father's passion was a dairy farm on the outskirts of the city. He appreciated the land, nature and creatures, that attitude transferred to his daughter at an early age. Her summertime visits and memories of her maternal grandparents' Michigan farm appeared in her last novel, *The Sojourner.*

Her parents encouraged Marjorie's precocious writing efforts that appeared in the *Washington Post,* children's page. Her interest in writing began early, about age six, but she did not win a prize for writing until age fifteen. She attended and graduated from the University of Wisconsin-Madison, majoring in English, in 1918. Marjorie's first job was in New York City with the YWCA, as an editor and writer. She met her husband, Charles Rawlings, at work, and they married a year later. They moved to Louisville, Kentucky, then back to Rochester, New York, near the home of the Rawlings family. Rochester Times-Union published, and syndicated in fifty other newspapers, Marjorie's very creative poetry, *Songs of a Housewife* for a total of 495 poems. Purpose was to acknowledge the contributions of housewives by illustrating that they were the glue keeping society together.

Both were disappointed with their writing careers. A turning point occurred in March 1928 while on a vacation near Ocala, Florida, visiting Charles's two brothers. Marjorie's fondness of natural beauty and the half-wild ethos of the simple life. Marjorie declared to her husband, "Let's sell everything and move South," states the Historic Record. The couple drove from Rochester, New York, in their Cadillac car, in

November 1928, to seventy- two acres they purchased in Cross Creek, with a small inheritance from her mother. Later, Marjorie purchased an additional 40 acres. The property consisted of 3,000 mature orange trees and 800 pecan trees.

The dilapidated frame vernacular farmhouse and barn needed the latest repairs. The structure consists of three separate units, probably added at different times, living, dining kitchen, and bedrooms connected by a breezeway, porches and bathroom. All spaces have cross-ventilation. Heating came from fireplaces and modern space heaters. The Rawlings brothers joined them in the management of the citrus grove and house repairs. The grove, across SR 325, produced six kinds of oranges, grapefruit and kumquats and was the main cash crop. Unfortunately, the

grove was lost to a freeze in 1983, long after Marjorie's death. She disliked the look of the leafless looking pecan trees and had them removed. The home is furnished with original house wares and furniture, Historic Record states.

The move to Florida revolutionized Marjorie's literary imagination. She filled journals "with detailed descriptions of flora and fauna, the delights of primitive rural lifestyle, and the portrayal of the local Florida Cracker Folks. Marjorie said, she felt vibrations from the land and she found her literary voice here. Her most productive years were at Cross Creek from 1930 to 1942.

Scribner's editor, Maxwell Perkins, encouraged her to write about Cross Creek ethos in the local discourse. The press valued her "regional literature." Her "literary works were written at the height of national interest in regionalism," Historic record states. Her early published short

Her first novel in 1933, *South Moon Under,* for background details Marjorie lived with a family in the wild Big Scrub, now Ocala National Forest. The family made and sold moonshine, illegally, and hunted for table food, illegally. Marjorie helped and related their activities in preparation for accuracy in writing the novel. Despite the depression years, her book sold sixty thousand copies in the first quarter of release. *South Moon Under* was a finalist for the Pulitzer Prize and included in the Book-of-the-Month-Club. Her principal editor, Max Perkins with Scribner's Publishing Firm, encouraged her to write about a young boy growing up in the Big Scrub.

Marjorie Rawlings produced her fourth novel in 1938, *The Yearling.* The book remained on the "best-seller list for ninety-three weeks and sold 240,000 copies in the first year. Most of the best books in the With her national celebrity, Marjorie entertained her new friends with her fine cooking at the farmhouse. Her great fondness for cooking lead her to publish

stories were, *Cracker Chidlings* and *Jacob's Ladder,* earned a $700 check, "which she used to install an indoor bathroom in the farmhouse" Historic Record states.

In 1933, Charles and Marjorie divorced; he did not find living in rural Florida attractive. City-bred Marjorie stayed on, lived alone in the country, with her back up, dependable help, Idella, *The Perfect Maid.* A hired hand took care of the grove. Marjorie Rawlings first commenced her writing career, publishing short stories for a total of twenty four and eleven novels.

world are read both by children and adults" Historic Record stated. A year later, *The Yearling* won the Pulitzer Prize and Rawlings was elected to the National Academy of Arts and Letters. Movie rights were sold to MGM but a delay occurred by World War II. By the end of 1942, "*The Yearling* was translated into thirteen foreign languages and was distributed, like *Cross Creek and South Moon Under* to thousands of servicemen in paperback" Historic Record states. Rawlings self-imposed isolation eased, as she found herself enjoying the company of many new author friends, Margaret Mitchell, Robert Frost, Wallace Stevens, James B. Cabell, and Zora Neale Hurston. Zora N. Hurston was often a guest in her home. Ernest Hemingway was her guest at the Crescent Beach home.

Cross Creek Cookery in 1942. Mouthwatering and delectable food descriptions included in her *Cross Creek* text, were examples of their community tastes. *Cross Creek* detailed over 100 of her community neighbors, some were delighted to be included. Later, in 1983 *Cross Creek* was make into a movie with actress Alfre Woodard being nominated for Best Supporting Actress.

One neighbor, Zelma Cason took exception and sued for "Invasion of Privacy" and demanded damages of $100,000. Rawlings was "convinced the principle of artistic freedom was at stake "and "felt duty-bound to defend the rights of all authors," Historic Record states. The case persisted for five years and was very disruptive to Rawlings's life in terms of time, money and emotion, but the jury brought in a verdict of "not guilty." The plaintiff appealed to the Florida Supreme Court and "the case dragged on. The final "judgment against the author was for a nominal sum of one dollar and court costs," Historic Record states. Marjorie was shocked that the case was ignored by the national press and in literary circles for she was fighting "for the basic freedom of the press." Tour guide stated, the legal case broke Rawlings's spirit.

In this time period, 1941, Marjorie Rawlings was married to Norton Baskin, a hotelier who remodeled and managed the Castle Warden Hotel (now the Ripley's Believe It or Not Museum) in St. Augustine. Marjorie divided her time between the resort city and her Cross Creek home. She required the Cross Creek quiet and isolation for her writing. World War II years hindered her writing. Her husband, Norton, was beyond draft age, but stationed overseas in Burma as an ambulance driver. She wrote to him daily. Depression and artistic frustration surfaced, so the next novel, *The Sojourner*, based on the life of her grandparents' farm in Michigan, was placed aside. First draft was submitted later in 1953. The sudden death of her editor, Maxwell Perkins in 1947 "was a devastating blow to Marjorie Rawlings." "As a protégé of Perkins, she belonged to a literary elite and moved easily in the company of these literary giants, becoming a national celebrity recognized for the timeless quality of her work," Historic Record states.

Rawlings died suddenly at Flagler Hospital in St. Augustine of a cerebral hemorrhage on December 12, 1953. She was buried at Antioch Cemetery near Island Grove, Florida; 44 years later her husband Norton joined her in the cemetery. Marjory Rawlings "bequeathed most of her property to the University of Florida, where she taught creative writing in Anderson Hall.

"The University honored her with a new dormitory dedicated in 1958 as Rawlings Hall." Wikipedia stated, Rawlings' Cross Creek Cracker style farm is now a Historic State Park, only a few of which remain in Florida, and is a National Landmark.

Rawlings' versatility as a writer lived on. She had three books published posthumously: *The Sojourn in 1953, The Secret River* and *Gal Young Un.* "Japanese critic Hisoshi Tsumemoto places Rawlings high, in the ranks of American writers who have taken nature and the environment as their themes–calling her "A Female Thoreau in Florida," comparable to Mark Twain, William Faulkner, and Henry D. Thoreau, Historic Record states. She was named A Great Floridian in 2009 by the state of Florida. This program honors persons who made "major contributions to the progress and welfare" of Florida.

To tour Marjorie Kinnan Rawlings Historic State Park, call (352) 466-3672 for time schedules, www.FloridaStateParks.org

RESEARCH STUDIO (MAITLAND ART CENTER)
Maitland, Florida
Orange County

National LANDMARK 2014

Roughly twenty miles across the city of Orlando from Disney World, the prosperous town of Maitland awaits your visit to its celebrated and acclaimed Maitland Art Center. "The Research Studio is a nationally significant example of Art Deco-Mayan Revival Architecture with embellishments, and is one of the most distinctively rendered sites of this style in the country," Record states. The Research Studio site at 231 West Packwood Avenue, designed by Architect J. Andre Smith, is in a layout of a cloister-like art village.

Andre Smith "born in 1880 in Hong Kong to American parents, raised in New York and Connecticut, and educated at Cornell University," received his Architecture degree in 1902 and Master's degree in 1904 from Cornell, Record states. Smith found success promptly. He received a gold medal for etching and "excelled in sculpture, painting and designing stage sets," Record states.

On a trip to Miami in the 1930's, Smith found Maitland. You can imagine the two-acre parcel with trees near the lake was very captivating for any buyer. Smith build his home on Packwood Avenue in Maitland. He became close friends with Annie Russell, Director of Theater at Rollins College, who introduced Smith to Mary Curtis Bok. Mary Bok was the well-funded daughter of Edward W. Bok, Developer of the Bok Singing Tower and former editor of Ladies Home Journal.

Bok and Smith agreed, the wealthy should invest in promising young American artists and modern art, not Italian primitive art. Mary Bok established the Research Studio Foundation, thus supporting Smith with his goals going forward. She assisted Smith with the purchase of adjacent land.

Architect, etcher, painter, author, Andre Smith designed his Art Deco residence in the early 1930's. The building served as a primary structure for the artists' village, which included six other principal buildings, several utility buildings, courtyards and ornamental pool of an artistic utopia. "All the buildings are one story with a flat roof. The exception was the gatehouse, gallery, and Bok Cottage Studio. "Each building is connected to another either physically with an adjoining wall, or visually by landscape elements and additions such as patios, pergolas, and pathways," Record states. On the north side of the walled structure are studio areas, reserved for visiting artists to experiment with their craft without interference. Each winter, the studio apartments included two to five visiting artists at the southeast corner of the Gallery," Record states. The buildings are grouped into two distinct areas and uses, with a large," grass-covered Central Courtyard and Pond as the unifying element." Buildings within this area are Andre Smith's, Director's Studio, his library (contains his 700 books), laundry, playroom, studio court

entrance and yard, artists in this communal arrangement. "All residing artists exhibited their works at the Research Studio gallery," Record states. Hosted artists included Ralston Crawford, Milton Avery, and Consuelo Kanaga. Today, these studios are "used for art classes or artist-in-residence programs." The artist village main compound is roughly 250 feet by 155 feet surrounded in this masonry maze-like walled site.

In 1942, an open air garden chapel was

constructed across Packwood Avenue to the west from the Research Studio. Natural canopy created by live oaks trees cradle the outdoor garden-like chapel. "Smith even arranged the tropical landscaping around the existed oak trees to shelter the compound and supply a garden and some exhibition spaces,"

Record states. The chapel is elevated by Smith's ornate sculptures and carved floor tiles. The chapel is utilized as a Wedding Venue. Can you imagine all the wedding photos framed with the prime art work in the background? Their website holds beautiful photos of many weddings with these striking backdrops. Smith dedicated the Chapel to his mother, who cared for him in 1924 after he had his leg amputated from a war wound. His mother's initials are carved into the angel praying hands of the crucifix.

The outdoor chapel is the cumulative of Smith's of architectual learning from his Ivy-

League education, his travels in Europe, his readings, and his "extensive knowledge of historic movements in art including Chinese, the Renaissance, Surrealism, and Aztec and Mayan Works," Record states.

Smith's distinctive architecture of Mayan Revival is also known as Fantasy artworks in the southeast.

Throughout, the Artist's Village and Garden Chapel Smith's Mayan-inspired bas reliefs demonstrates his talent and flair. His designed relief ornaments covers the interior and exterior walls. Smith developed a new techniques using cast cement. Smith developed a new techniques using cast cement. "His method was to carve and mold designs in cements slabs, before they hardened, using grapefruit knives, teaspoons, and brush handles. The medallions, bas reliefs, sculptures and cement grillwork, --- animals, birds, and plants -- are represented in the compound walls," Records states. Many of the bas-reliefs were painted in brilliant colors. The predominant theme has an Aztec-Mayan motif of stylized faces with fancy costumes, Japanese influences, pagan idols, and Buddhist and Christian themes.

The Maitland Art Center enjoys international recognition. "In 1957 an English publication, *The Voice,* labeled the Center one of the 15 most beautiful examples of architecture in the world," Record states. Smith's period of significance was from the site's construction in 1934 to his death in 1959. Delicate preservation continues, with the "Art and History non-profit organization funded by earned income to the City of Maitland, State of Florida, United Arts of Central Florida, grants, and individual donations," Maitland Website states. The contact number is (407) 539-2181 x 253.

SAFETY HARBOR SITE

2355 Bayshore Drive
Pinellas County
National Landmark 1964

The townsfolks may relate to this site as Philippe Park. Safety Harbor was a culture site of the Tocobaga Natives. Pinellas County purchased the site in 1948 and excavations begun.

Overlooking the west shore of Old Tampa Bay, Safety Harbor Site is located on Philippe Point. The village site was occupied by Tocobaga Indians between A.D. 1400 and 1700. The Safety Harbor group and Timucua tribe "probably occupied an area from Charlotte Harbor on the south to the Aucilla River in the north and in Pinellas County," Record states. European explorers describe the Tocobago Indians as "very tall, (5'9), "in comparison to Spanish and European height of (5'2"), more or less. Tocobaga existed in a class society. The higher rank chief lived on the large temple mound overlooking the water, the best spot. Class status was based on a "combination of their birthright, their wealth, and their abilities as a warrior," Record states. What happened to the Tocobago tribe? Diseases brought by the Europeans, smallpox and tuberculosis did much killing. Native Americans had no immunity to these diseases. Wars killed many. Records suggest, Natives were skilled warriors with spears, bows and arrows. Tocobaga bows were so strong, the Spanish could not draw them back.

Creek tribe from South Georgia and any remnants of Tocobaga may have joined them. Writings suggest the village was visited by Pedro Mendenez in 1567, a short time after Florida was discovered by Ponce de Leon. Mendenez held a detail of soldiers at the site for several months.

Native's water source came from the springs from the edges of the park. Food sources came from a combination of agriculture, hunting for small game and fishing. Deer, fish bones and shell material were found in the middens.

"The Safety Harbor Site includes a platform mound, about 70 feet square and approximately 20 feet high. Some believe the hugh mound was "the capital of the Tocobaga chiefton. " Another mound theory, it was a temple, as the square shape suggests. The burial mound is 80 feet in diameter and 12 feet high and found holding more than 100 burials, as excavated by M. Stirling in 1929.

After the Pinellas County purchased the site in 1948, Florida Park Service laborers worked under the " direction of R.Bullen and J. Griffin investigating in three area: the large mound, small mound southwest of the large mound, small mound to the northwest of large mound," Record States. The team discovered the large mound was in "various stages of construction." The stages were layers of clay and sand. The clay floors capped the sand and this expanded the structure. Southwest mound was natural sand deposit. Northwest mound yielded post holes and pits with no pattern recognized. Additional artifacts found at

Geography of the original inhabitants of the lower Southeast.

the site reveal Safety Harbor type pottery called Pinellas Plain vessels.

"Vessels are large open bowls with slightly incurbate rims, casuella bowls, collared pot forms," Record states. "Glades pottery from the south is common at the site, and St. Johns sherds indicating contacts to the east have also been recovered," Historic Record states.

Ship wreck off the coast conveyed mirages of a hidden, vast treasure buried in the large Indian mound. In 1949, investigations began a search with a powerful metal detector. "The result of the investigation was, there was no positive indication of buried metal in the mound. This was obtained under the conditions demonstrated by the treasure hunters," Record states.

Pinellas County in 10/11/19 listed five new Archaeological sites on the National Register of Historic Places. The writer does not have the site addresses. All interested parties should contact Pinellas County Planner for the addresses.

ST. AUGUSTINE TOWN PLAN HISTORIC DISTRICT

St. Augustine, Florida
St. Johns County
National Landmark 1970

Contrary to what many believe, Florida is not a young state. In 2020 Florida will be 507 years old. St. Augustine was established in 1565, forty-two years before Jamestown, Virginia. St. Augustine is the oldest city in America, reflecting Florida's Spanish heritage.

St. Augustine is believed to be the first master-planned community in North America, as founded by the Spanish in 1565. "Law of the Indies" document set the rules the Spanish Crown issued in the 16th, 17th, and 18th centuries for government, to guide development and solve issues. The key doctrine is the common area or "town plaza" to be built in the center of the community. The purpose of the town plaza was to have sufficient space where the people may go for recreation and "take their cattle to pasture without them causing any damage". All buildings were expected to be of "one type for the beauty of the town" or a collective architecture type of houses. Around the town plaza is the government building and across the town plaza is the church, along with the public space. The two themes, "the military and religion," dominated this historic period, 1565 to 1763.

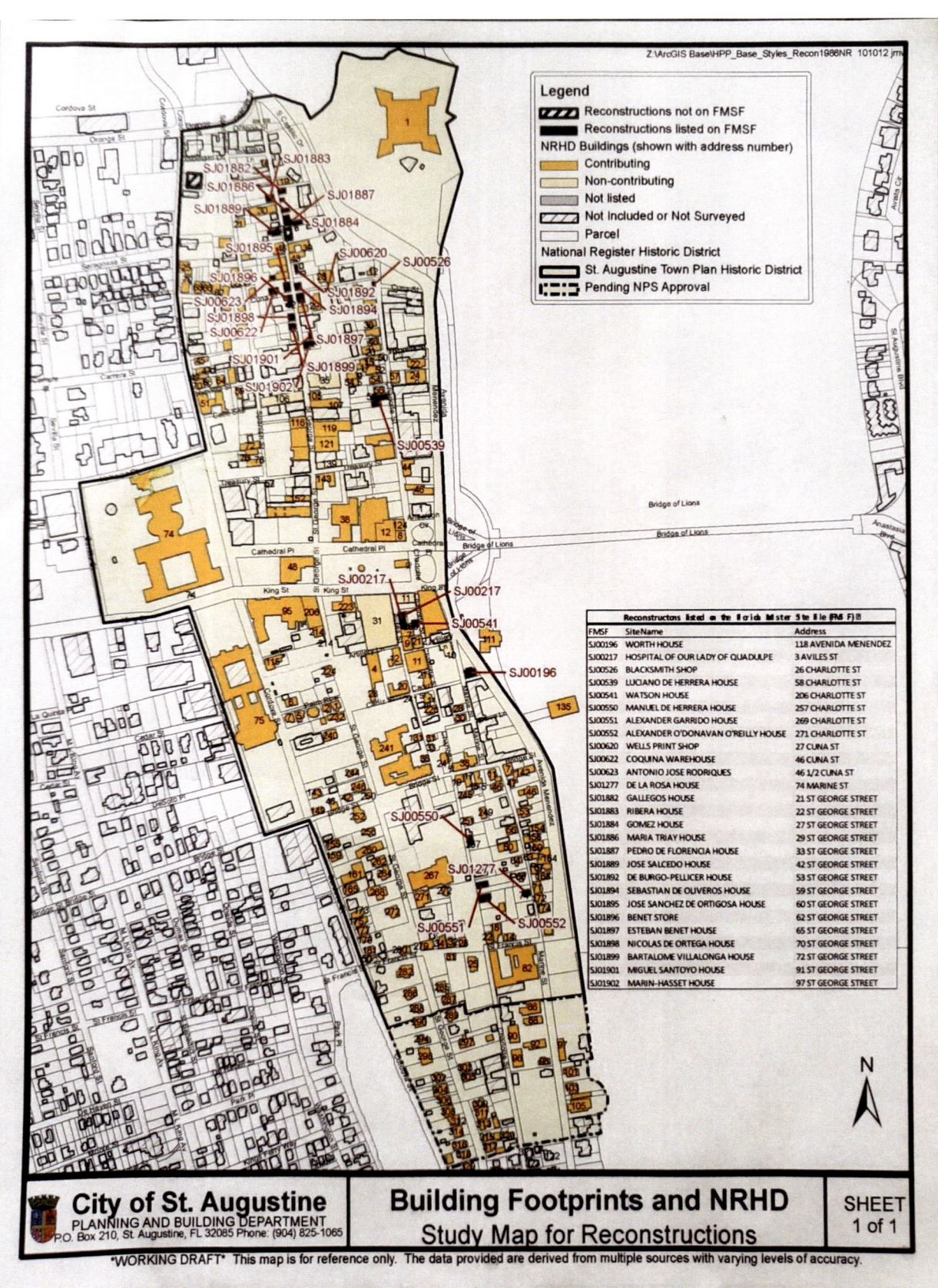

Fort Castillo de San Marcos is the largest building in St. Augustine and now a major tourist attraction. Construction began in 1672 and completed in 1756. Coquina shell walls are twelve feet thick at the base, but tapered to seven feet at the upper defensive wall. Castillo held against James Moore, British Governor of Carolina. Three signers of the Declaration of Independence were detained at the fort. The fort served as a military prison during the Second Seminole, Civil, and Spanish-American Wars. The Castillo is classified as a National Monument in 1924, but remains in St Augustine Historic District.

Next to the Castillo and the next line of defense was the St. Augustine Gate, the north end of St. George Street. Near the gate is the Oldest School House, 14 St. George Street, and is believed to be oldest wooden school building in the United States. The exact date of construction is not known. The wooden walls are cypress and red cedar and held together by wooden pins and iron spikes.

From the central town plaza, principal streets were laid out in a grid pattern of narrow streets that provided shade in hot climates. St. George Street became the first street oriented for trading and crafts and became the commerce center. Surrounding the central town plaza is the Cathedral Parish Church, oldest Catholic structure in the United States, established in 1594. Cathedral of St. Augustine is a National Historic Landmark with a supporting chapter in this book.

Flags changed to the British in 1763 to 1783 and returned to Spanish control in 1783, then to the United States in 1821. Economic boom in the early territorial periods never really occurred or was short-lived. Inadequate system of transportation proved to be a major obstacle to the economic development of St. Augustine. Roughly in 1883, a new railroad line from Jacksonville acted as a catalyst for the revitalization of the city. The economy and the tourist trade flourished.

Boom time arrived when Henry M. Flagler visited St. Augustine in 1880's. The excellent climate stimulated his new vision of the "Ancient City becoming the Winter Newport," a resort center for wealthy northerners. Flagler constructed two major hotels in St. Augustine, the Ponce de Leon and Alcazar, and purchased a third, the Cordova, to add to his complex," states the Historic Record. Presently, the Ponce de Leon Hotel is Flagler College. Many architectural significant structures in the district date from the Flagler boom period,

1890 to 1895. In 1895 a fierce freeze devastated the citrus industry in North Florida, and Henry Flagler moved south with his railroad and hotel developments. "St. Augustine continued attracting tourists and winter residents at a steady unspectacular rate. The local tourist industry prospered during World War I, as

many wealthy tourists who previously traveled overseas instead came to St. Augustine and Florida," Historic Record states. During the Boom time, "the Atlantic National Bank Building, the only true skyscraper in the Ancient City, was build," Record states. Economic development proceeded with the construction of the Dixie Highway linking St. Augustine to Jacksonville, making progress for a better transportation system to the city during the Florida Land Boom following World War I.

"St. Augustine Historic District is significant for its architecture, spanning the period 1672 to 1935," Record states. After the Spanish Colonial period architecture, other styles came forward, as with Flagler's Ponce de Leon Hotel, Spanish Renaissance style. Distinctive styles include Carpenter Gothic, Second Empire, Moorish Revival, the Queen Anne, Colonial Revival, Spanish Revival, and the Bungalow. Several architects, Alexander J. Davis, Mariano de la Rocque, James Renwick and Franklin W. Smith succeeded with their designs in St. Augustine. A. Davis's work is represented in the district by the Bronson Cottage at 252 St. George Street. In 1594, M. de la Rocque designed the Parish Cathedral. A fire in 1887 gutted the roof and interior of the church, leaving only the stone walls standing. A long time winter resident of the ancient city, James Renwick restored and enlarged the structure. Renwick added a six-story bell-tower with a tall steeple to the west, with a two-story connection to the main building. In the rear, Renwick expanded the building by 4,000 feet by adding large east and west wings. Financial assistance was provided by Henry Flagler who was building his grand hotels. Franklin W. Smith designed the Cordova Hotel (originally the Casa Monica), and his work is acclaimed in St. Augustine.

"The origin of the plan dates back to 1936, when the Carnegie Institution of Washington, D.C., and St. Augustine city leaders devised a plan to restore the colonial city. Mayor Walter Fraser favored a Williamsburg approach to recreate the colonial city, while John C. Merriam, President of Carnegie Institution, proposed a selective restoration program based on substantial research," Record states. Verne Chatelain resigned from the National Park Service, and headed up the work program in St. Augustine. Chatelain's theory was not to "freeze history" to a target date because the "restoration program must emphasize the idea of a "living city" that had developed over many years," Record states.

Funding for the preservation work in St. Augustine was hard to come by for the restoration commitment that was made in 1930s. "Carnegie Institution's leadership changed and their support for the St. Augustine project that was severely cut," Record states. Governor Leroy Collins started the challenge and appointed the special State Commission. "The Restoration program began in 1959 when the Florida Legislature passed an act establishing the St. Augustine Historical Restoration and Preservation Commission. " In 1962 a private non-profit organization, St. Augustine Restoration Inc., was formed to assist the State Commission," Record states.

In support of the project, "the University of Florida proposed a partnership with the City

Flagler's Burial Site, Presbyterian Church of St. Augustine. The local host government developed a master plan for historic St. Augustine, identifying the original town plan, significant buildings and sites, pedestrian and traffic circulation, parking, wayfinding through the historic area. Funding request was $500,000" Historic Record states.

Florida Department of State, Division of Historical Resources, Florida Master Site File
Building Summary and Budget Estimate

BLDG	NAME	ADDRES	GSF	YR	MAINTENANCE	$/SQ FT	RENOVATION	$/SQ FT
3900	GOVERNMENT HOUSE	48 KING STREET	25,947	1710			$ 14,271,000	$ 550
3901	DE MESA SANCHEZ HOUSE	49 ST. GEORGE STREET	4,068	1760	$ 25,000	$ 6		
3902	ARRIVAS HOUSE	46 ST. GEORGE STREET	4,041	1961	$ 885,000	$ 219		
3903	PAREDES DODGE HOUSE	54 ST. GEORGE STREET	1,392	1808			$ 1,325,000	$ 952
3904	PAREDES DODGE OUTBUILDING	54 1/2 ST. GEORGE STREET	231	1808				
3905	GALLEGOS HOUSE	21 ST. GEORGE STREET	905	1963	$ 198,000	$ 219		
3906	RIBERA HOUSE	22 ST. GEORGE STREET	2,168	1964	$ 271,000	$ 125		
3907	RIBERA KITCHEN	22 ST. GEORGE STREET	480	1964	$ 85,500	$ 178		
3908	TRIAY HOUSE	29 ST. GEORGE STREET	690	1964	$ 106,875	$ 155		
3909	GOMEZ HOUSE	27 ST. GEORGE STREET	314	1964	$ 57,750	$ 184		
3910	CERVEAU HOUSE	26 CUNA STREET	3,059	1885			$ 1,682,000	$ 550
3911	HAAS HOUSE	28 CUNA STREET	2,337	1850	$ 511,000	$ 219		
3912	PESO DE BURGO / PELLICER HOUSE	53 ST. GEORGE STREET	682	1976	$ 340,750	$ 499		
3913	PESO DE BURGO N OUTBUILDING	53 ST. GEORGE STREET	337	1976	$ 54,750	$ 163		
3914	PESO DE BURGO S OUTBUILDING	53 ST. GEORGE STREET	260	1976	$ 56,875	$ 218		
3915	JOANEDA HOUSE	57 TREASURY STREET	1,424	1806	$ 178,000	$ 125		
3916	RODRIGUEZ HOUSE	46 1/2 CUNA STREET	714	1966	$ 22,300	$ 31		
3917	BENET HOUSE	65 ST. GEORGE STREET	2,706	1965	$ 84,500	$ 31		
3918	COQUINA HOUSE	46 CUNA STREET	2,270	1966	$ 196,875	$ 87		
3919	SANCHEZ DE ORTIGOSA HOUSE	60 ST. GEORGE STREET	1,172	1965	$ 250,000	$ 213		
3920	DE HITA HOUSE	37 ST. GEORGE STREET	638	1979	$ 99,750	$ 156		
3921	GONZALEZ HOUSE	39 ST. GEORGE STREET	519	1979	$ 32,500	$ 63		
3922	NEW BLACKSMITH SHOP	37 1/2 ST. GEORGE STREET	242	1983	$ 30,250	$ 125		
3923	FLORENCIA HOUSE	33 ST. GEORGE STREET	2,105	1965	$ 460,500	$ 219		
3924	SPANISH MILITARY HOSPITAL	2 AVILES STREET	3,522	1965	$ 220,000	$ 62		
3925	WATSON HOUSE	206 CHARLOTTE STREET	2,161	1965	$ 270,000	$ 125		
3926	SALCEDO KITCHEN	42 1/2 ST. GEORGE STREET	563	1962	$ 52,750	$ 94		
3927	SALCEDO HOUSE	42 ST. GEORGE STREET	2,191	1962	$ 274,000	$ 125		
3928	GONZALEZ RESTROOMS	35 1/2 ST. GEORGE STREET	182	1983	$ 24,000	$ 132		
3929	SIMS HOUSE	12 CUNA STREET	802	1964	$ 125,500	$ 155		
3930	SIMS OUTBUILDING	12 CUNA STREET	173	1964	$ 22,000	$ 127		
3931	OLD BLACKSMITH SHOP	26 CHARLOTTE STREET	363	1966	$ 117,250	$ 323		
3932	HARNESS SHOP	17 CUNA STREET	566	1967	$ 106,000	$ 187		
3933	PUBLIC RESTROOMS	40 ST. GEORGE STREET	624	1966	$ 78,000	$ 125		
		TOTAL ESTIMATED FUNDING REQUIRED:	69,848	GSF	$ 5,236,675		$ 17,278,000	
		GRAND TOTAL REQUESTED FOR DEFERRED MAINTENANCE AND RENOVATIONS:					$ 22,514,675	
		AMOUNT REQUESTED THROUGH LEGISLATIVE BUDGET REQUEST FOR PO&M FUNDING ($7/SQ FT):					$ 488,937	

The attached "document is intended to be a general assessment of 34 State-owned buildings in the City of St. Augustine that are potentially being turned over to the University of Florida for initial rehabilitation, future operations and maintenance. A team of University professionals included representatives from the Division of Facilities, Planning and Construction, Physical Plant, and Environmental Health and Safety." These teams "spent over 300 hours evaluating structures, finishes, utilities infrastructure, life and fire safety, and ADA accessibility." For the purpose of "initial costs necessary to bring the structures up to current codes and standards, and allowing for continued maintenance," Record states.

The Restoration Program began in 1960's. The Government Building is the best example of a concluded work. This building at 48 King Street, built in 1710 was "completely rebuilt in 1937," with the exception of the East Wing coquina walls, which date from the Colonial Era. "Renovation cost estimate was $14,271,000 for the 25,947 gross square feet. Americans with Disabilities Act, ADA included 12 recommendations to complete in the Government Building along with roof damage and other upgrades," Record states. University of Florida, is managing the 34 State-owned sites. The St. Augustine local contact manager is Billy Triay (btriay@UFL.edu) from the Government House and within UF the manager is Linda Dixon, (ldixon@UFL.edu).

You should tour south on St. George Street for a pleasant and extensive appreciation of Spanish Historic Residential homes, Colonel Upham, Bronson, and Stansbury dwellings. In St. Augustine 2020, the Spanish model is still present and preserved for all the locals and tourist to appreciate and enjoy, and have prosperity for many years. Another symbol of St. Augustine, not in the Historic District, is the Lions Bridge, built in 1926 and designed to complement the downtown architecture. Tourist love the photo spot location for a city remembrance of the stately marble lions on the bridge. Appreciation attracts appreciation.

SAN LUIS de TALIMALI

Tallahassee, Florida
Leon County

NATIONAL LANDMARK 1960

The rolling hills of Tallahassee create breathe taking beauty. Alluring natural beauty is often missing from other regions of Florida. Prior to 1824, Florida had two capitals, Pensacola and St. Augustine. Traveling between two towns created difficulty, so the territorial legislature sought a middle ground. The favorable solution was moving the capital to the hilly, half-way point, Tallahassee. Florida's capital city represents separate numerous regions and cultures. In this idyllic setting with rich soils, one can comprehend why the ancestors Apalache nation made the area their central region villages.

On the fringes of Tallahassee, San Luis was the largest Spanish Mission supported by a large Native Apalache population, and recognized as the provincial capital, during the late seventeenth century. Records report, "Friars made a first friendly visit to the Apalachee in 1608." Later, 1633, or (1656) Spanish Franciscans Friars established the Mission of San Luis. The first deputy Apalache governor was appointed in 1645. "Non-Christian Indians staged an uprising in 1647, where seven of the eight existing churches were destroyed and the deputy governor, his family, and three friars were killed." In 1656 San Luis was recognized as the provincial capital and a large native population moved to the location. The capital was established on the region's highest hilltops for strategic

defense methods. "From 1656 to 1704 San Luis was the capital of some fourteen missions (Apalache) towns and approximately thirty satellite villages," Record states.

The Spanish command referred to the Mission San Luis as its western capital, as a social, administrative, religious, and military capital. In 1693 British traders stirred up back-country Creek tribes. Spanish defenses were strengthen by erecting a "large wooden blockhouse (fort) with a moat" and fortified by 40 soldiers. "The fort and mission served as headquarters for seven missionary settlements, with a population of more than fifteen hundred people," Florida Forts states. At this time San Luis de Talimali, first appeared in Spanish documents.

The importance of San Luis for the Spanish was the area served as a "breadbasket" for the St. Augustine Mission that also shipped food to Havana. With the fertile soils, San Luis Apalache Indians were enlisted and recruited for labor projects. Women were "excellent agriculturists," the food gatherings, the farmers, the food preparers. Men hunted wild game, and fought in wars. Children worked alongside the adults to learn everyday skills. "The 63-acre site is characterized as prime agricultural land with Orangeburg soils with seep springs that run year-round," Record states.

Apalache society was well-organized by "chiefs" and guided by Franciscan priests. An Apalache family places more importance on the mother's relatives than the father's kin, which is the custom in Europe. This custom granted more cultural status to Apalache women than European women. When a couple link (marry), they live with the wife's mother's family.

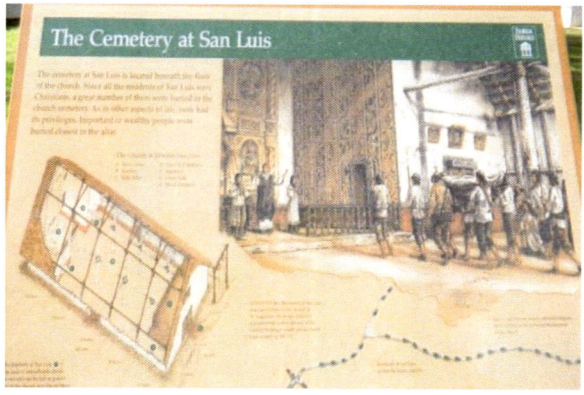

"War broke out between Britain and Spain in 1702," according to History of Florida Forts. In January 1704, "Governor James Moore led his South Carolinians and Creek Indians into Apalache (country) to crush the Spanish power," Record states. San Luis held. Some Apalache were captured, tortured, burned at the stake, and made an example for unconditional surrender. Atrocities strong in their memory, some Apalache agreed to relocate to the Carolina territory. A second Indian force arrived in June 1704 to destroy the remaining missions, but leaving only San Luis in existence. The remaining population sought refuge within San Luis stockade. Spaniards and the natives heard of a rumored third attack. Together, the two groups, Spanish and Apalache resolved to

abandon the territory. They evacuated San Luis in July and destroyed the village, fort, blockhouse by fire. "The Spanish families withdrew to Pensacola by ship; the garrison and some natives retreated overland toward St. Augustine," Record states. Other natives led the way toward Pensacola by land, then on to Mobile that was recently established by the French. Neither the Spanish nor Apalache returned to occupy San Luis again.

"A year after the evacuation of San Luis, Admiral Antonio de Landeche sailed into Apalache Bay to the San Luis Site with 180 men. He found no people, and only an unburned part of the stockade still standing," Record states. He carefully described and mapped the area and his records still exist.

Later Seminole Indians arrived and took advantage of the Apalache fields, but avoided the mission ruins, the broken cannon and church remains. "Mission San Luis was never lost to Tallahassee residents" and fort remnants were visible until 1820. "Three founding fathers of Florida archaeology: John Griffin, (1948), Hale Smith, (1950), and Charles Fairbanks, (1956 & 1957), each worked at the fort in attempts to define basic features," Record states. Since the evacuation a series of owners of the site existed. First owners were Robert Jameson and Benjamin Clements in 1825 and use was not stated. Second owner A.M. Randolph, (1855-1864), as part of his 800 plus acre plantation. Frenchman Emile DuBois started a vineyard (1884-1890). "In 1932, James Messer purchased 362 acres that included the 50 acres of San Luis and his heirs sold the land to the State of Florida in 1983. Messer's family home, two story mansion on site serves as the Visitors Center that is open to the public.

Reconstruction of the Apalache mission began with archaeological digs, research and field investigations on the 63 acre site approximately 1985. The first Director of Archaeology was Dr. Gary Shapiro, and Dr. John Hann was the site historian. San Luis was the largest council house reconstructed with a direct correlation between a village population and the size of the council house; built to hold between 2000 and 3000 people. Council house served as a political, social, (nightly dances), lodges for visitors, ritual functions, such as pre-ballgame ceremonies (La Crosse games) and brewing, drinking *cacina*, (made from cocoa and chocolate). Village council house symbolized the bond of the community." Council House was the "property of the chief and symbol of his authority that held his people together", Record states. The thatched structure held a large opening in the center of the roof for the smoke to escape. A company, Ace Thatch & Bamboo in Clermont, Florida, endorsed the Zulu warriors from South Africa to complete the roof thatching, using palm fronds. These fronds are nailed one by one into the wood poles, thus giving a cone-shaped building form, and from the ground up to 43 feet to the hole in the center. Archaeologists worked with architects to confirm the project's original work met current state codes. The council house's interior is furnished with two concentric rows of wooden benches that serve as beds and seats called niches or *barbacoas*. The chief's higher central platform is located upwards from floor level and behind the central hearth.

The Chief's house is in close proximity to the Council House. The thatched circular structure with a large central hearth, measures "78 feet in diameter" and approximately three times the size other Apalache houses. The archaeology digs revealed the "waster ground soil contained few European items, although cow and pig remains were identified. Digs uncovered "the chiefly residence was a pottery manufacturing area, concentration of Apalachee materials across this area appears to have resulted from native activities," Record states. A large number of quartz crystal beads and pendants were recovered. This reflects the chief's authority of dual religious and political values.

On the Town Plaza across from the imposing Council House, there was meticulous reconstruction of the religious complex located, west of the plaza. The massive church complex included the friars' residence, a detached kitchen, a cemetery, (located in the church floor). The church "towering forty-five feet from the floor to the thatched roof peak". As the western capital, "the San Luis Church was comparable in size to its counterpart in St. Augustine (approximately 110 feet long by 50 feet wide)," Record states. Religious conversion of the Apalache transformed change. "The Apalaches requested friars, accepted the Catholic faith voluntarily, and were described as being "thoroughly Christianized," Record states. Native cemetery burials, and the service were almost purely in Christian fashion. Researchers "reflect only the skeletal remains of the Apalaches are buried in the cemetery. Today, no Europeans have been identified in the San Luis cemetery, suggesting the Spanish population chose to be transported back to St. Augustine for burial near their families," Record states. The church was the center of many other fundamental social life changes, marriage, holidays, and education. "The Church and Crown encouraged intermarriage as a means of civilizing the native populations. Apalache women accepted marriage to Spaniards as a form of upward mobility for themselves and their *mestizos* children, who were exempt from manual labor," Record states. During the writer's visit, the church was closed to visitors because of a Bat infestation. Doors were open for a visional inspection. The immense sanctuary with high walls was decorated with large paintings; statues generated a peaceful haven of safety.

The blockhouse and fort dominated the north side of the hill, which was the highest point and over-looked and protected the entire community. A protected trench called a "covered way" led to the freshwater springs. Spanish authorities began construction in 1695 and completed the complex in 1697. "Blockhouse measured 85 feet by 58 feet. " The roof was covered with doubled planks to support four-pound cannons, one in each corner. The Military Complex was "protected by a twelve-foot-high stockade with a moat in front. The stockade measured 230.1 feet by 131 feet and erected around the church and convent for protection," Record states.

"San Luis de Apalache" name was used in the original designation, as a generic name from the 1655 list of missions. San Luis de Talimali remained until the mission was destroyed in 1704. The documentation was updated in 2004 and the correct name applied. "The 63-acre site is the only reconstructed 17th century Spanish mission in Florida. San Luis is located within the city limits of Tallahassee and the

Department of State manages the site."

Mission San Luis Apalache located in 1704 to Mobile, Alabama. In 1763, most of these Apalaches relocated to Rapides Parish, Louisiana. Today, only 250 to 300 of the Talimali Band of the Apalache are the only documented descendants of the native population of Florida.

The ethos of the reconstructed 17th century Spanish westernmost capital mission offers a living history. Opportunities enable an escape to another time, talk to the Friar at the church, hear the ring of the blacksmith's hammer, smell traditional foods being cooked over an open fire, walk the plaza where the Apalaches played their traditional ball games, see costumed living interpreters, hands on exhibits about a soldier's life at the fort, explore 300-year old archaeological artifacts and walk the plaza. The exceptional community where Apalachee Indians and Spanish newcomers lived together, a superb illustration. For contact information and special programs, you can call (850) 245-6406 or go to MissionSanLuis.org.

TAMPA BAY HOTEL

401 West Kennedy Boulevard
Tampa, Florida
Hillsborough County

National Landmark 1976

Henry Bradley Plant is known as the "Father of Tampa". He extended his railroad to Tampa in 1884. This stimulated rapid growth and changed a sleepy fishing village with a population of 720 to the robust city of today. The Tampa Bay Hotel is an exotic, precious jewel, Tampa's first national landmark.

Landmark designation by the Secretary of Interior is given to historic sites that are of outstanding value and quality in illustrating the heritage of our nation. Tampa Bay Hotel holds a twofold significance. First, the hotel served as headquarters for the army that invaded Cuba during the Spanish-American War. The conflict clearly established the United States as a world power. Second, the hotel is symbolic of early efforts that opened Florida for development by railroad and attracted tourist.

The imposing Tampa Bay Hotel, in a Moorish Revival design, is eccentric looking, not only in Florida, but in our country. Moorish Revival style is used most often with an acceptable, artistic blend of many other elements. The masterful New York Architect, J.A. Wood, designed the imposing Moorish Revival style in brick, four-story structure with 13 minarets towers, topped in crescent moon finials, supported by silver onion shaped domes. Window construction

State Archives: Henry Plant

is accented with chrysanthemum shapes and framed in Victorian gingerbread grillwork. Many original French imported glass windows are still in place.

The interior rooms feature many exceptional spaces. The Solarium, a large circular room between the lobby and dining room, is filled with tropical plants and sun light. The ballroom, or the music room as students now call it, has a distinctive domed ceiling. Records state the hotel was the first electrified building, interior and exterior, in the state. The hotel's cost was $3,000,000, including building and furnishings.

Two thousand people were invited to the grand opening on February 5, 1891. Henry Plant invited many honored guests, and also included his rival, Henry Flagler. Flagler wired back, "Where's Tampa?" Plant's reply, "Just follow the crowd." Records state that Flagler did attend. Guests were greeted by the Albert Opera Company performing "Faust."

During the hotel's first season 4287 registered guests enjoyed the health resort which combined an atmosphere of elegance and serenity with a balmy winter climate. Tampa Bay Hotel provided the same amenities as other Gilded Age hotels but with one addition. Plant provided good music and excellent plays for his guests, as he also enjoyed them.

Plant cleverly engaged prominent New York performers, John Drew, Anna Pavlova, Sarah Bernhardt, and Paderewski, who were in route to Cuba. He convinced the stars to stop in Tampa to perform for his hotel guests.

Plant's goal was to open Florida's west coast, as Henry Flagler did on the east coast. Plant gained prominence in Florida for the 600 miles of railroads under his control. His steamboat routes ran from New York to Havana and other ports on the Gulf coast of Florida. He owned seven hotels along the Gulf coast, and in central Florida. Plant's enterprises operated parallel to Henry Flagler's operations. Plant and Flagler were contemporaries. Both introduced railroads and luxury resorts, which were built far from the beaches. Plant and Flagler consolidated their steamship companies to form the Peninsula and Occidental Steamship Company. Both held equal shares and agreed to expand their services.

In 1899, Henry Plant passed away. Six years later Plant's heirs sold the beautiful Tampa Bay Hotel to the City of Tampa for $125,000 dollars. Lease holder, W. F. Adams, prospered, operating the hotel until the Florida Real Estate boom collapsed in 1927. Adams declared bankruptcy in 1932.

In 1933, the owner, City of Tampa, offered to lease the hotel site for $1 a year, to the University of Tampa. At the time the University functioned as a two-year junior college, but soon established a four-year program. The immense hotel structure, with over 511 rooms, was the main facility for the university and is now titled Plant Hall. Today, the University holds ownership. It has fondly preserved and transformed the building by restoring corridors, and adapting suites for new uses.

On the south wing ground floor, the Plants maintained a private apartment that is now Henry Plant Museum. The museum exhibits many original imported, exotic hotel furnishings and is a must see. Contact information is 813-254-1891, www.plantmuseum.com, and www.tampapreservation.com.

VIZCAYA

Miami
Miami-Dade County, Florida

National Landmark 1994

Vizcaya means "an elevated place." "President Ronald Regan entertained Pope John Paul II at Vizcaya in 1987. Seven years later, in 1994, President Bill Clinton hosted the Summit of the Americas" at Vizcaya, states Douglas Waitley, *Florida History from the Highways.* Leaders from thirty-four hemispheric nations created 'Free Trade Area of the Americas (FTAA).' Additional visiting dignitaries included Queen Elizabeth II, King Juan Carlos and Queen Sofia of Spain.

These grand representations are impressive visits to Vizcaya. The Deering family moved from South Paris, Maine, to Evanston, Illinois, where his father built a factory to manufacture farm machinery. "James

Deering was educated at Northwestern University and the Massachusetts Institute of Technology and then entered the family business." In 1902 the firm merged with McCormick Harvester Company ---to form the International Harvester Company. James Deering was the firm's vice-president until 1919 when he resigned, however he continued to serve as director to the time of his death in 1925, "Historic Record states.

Deering pursued his philanthropic interests and traveled extensively. From his travels he considered other warm weather locations, but he choose Miami as the best setting to build his house. "He suffered from pernicious anemia, a disease little understood at that time; his doctors

advised him to spend the winter months in a warm climate," Historic Record states.

Deering's land purchase was originally 180 acres of coast line in Coconut Grove as his working farm, called a "village." The large land purchase was from the pioneer Miami family, Mrs. William Brickell. Today, the estate is much smaller, (50 acres including Vizcaya Village).

Elsie de Wolfe of New York Studio of Interior Decoration introduced James Deering to Paul Chalfin, a New York painter and designer who attended Harvard and studied in France and Italy.

Deering and Chalfin traveled to Europe to observe domestic architecture, art and furniture design. Both, Deering and Chalfin preferred the country houses of Italian Vento, northern Italy, and the area. Deering lacked art collector skills. For the final selections, he depended on advice from Chalfin. Chalfin was not a trained architect, but he referred Francis Burrall Hoffman, a graduate of Harvard who also had a diploma from Ecole des Beaux Arts in Paris.

Deering had confirmed his preferred choice was Italian Mediterranean style of architecture with the expectation the style would be suitable for his Florida house. Hoffman began his drawings for the Deering house while visiting the Miami site in 1913. In that year Hoffman traveled to observe the villas of Italy for himself.

Hoffman's architectural villa master plan retained a panoramic view of Biscayne Bay, beginning with the design of ornamental Great Stone Barge which serves as a break water. The barge conveys a sense of calm and beauty. Barge's sculptural elements were designed by Stirling Calder. At the south end of the Venetian Bridge is the lattice-domed Tea house. Deering enjoyed receiving his guests' arrivals at the Stone Barge for the lavish parties.

The elegant, showplace main house construction began in 1914, and became the jewel of South Florida. "Stonecutters were imported from Italy and technicians from Scotland, in addition to 1,000 Miamians work force," J.P.Morris, *Florida Place Names*. The house contains 45,225-square feet in 34 decorated rooms in the main house. When James Deering was in town, he visited the site every day. His workers called him, "Mr. Jimmy." The exterior construction was reinforced concrete walls, stuccos, red roof tiles, and painted in pale shades of yellow and oranges. The Italian Renaissance palace style held open loggias and arcades with native coral ornamentation. The interiors are filled with priceless paintings, tapestries and period furniture, gathered from the grand palaces of Europe. Each space is embellished with refined silks, ornate brackets and beams, hand-crafted tiles, doors and their gilding surrounds, decorative chimney-pieces and mantles that are all symbolic of Deering's travels with Chalfin.

The third Deering associate, landscape architect Diego Suarez, was commissioned to design Vizcaya's gardens. Suarez was born in Bogota, Colombia, but educated in Florence, Italy, as an architect but had a predilection for landscape design. He met with Deering while working on a historic villa being restored La Pietra, near Florence, Italy.

Vizcaya's main garden design is in a fan-shaped plan, "based on a Renaissance and Baroque designs inspired by Suarez' extensive knowledge of Italian gardens, -- and applicable to the architectural design that applies to the house." "With the interruption of World War I, it took seven years (1922) for these gardens to be completed in Suarez' designs, " Historic Record states.

"To the west--- lay the farm section of the estate with buildings designed by Architect Hoffman to resemble a small northern Italian village. Here lived the resident estate superintendent, chief engineer, boat captain, boat engineer, garage supervisor, poultry man, and the fishing guide, as well, as other key personnel. Along with garages and workshops, there were stables, a cow barn, a diary and a poultry house. A pump

house provided water for extensive flower and vegetable gardens. There was a greenhouse and a large shade house for delicate plants.

Lattice Tea House

Pineapple, citrus and fruits were grown. The estate could be nearly self-sufficient. Electricity for power and light came from Miami. Telephone service went to all parts of the estate, through its own switchboard. "The major buildings of the Farm Village remain today and are restored as part of Vizcaya's museum complex," Historic Record states. "Today, there are periodic tours of the Vizcaya Village and various programs for school children, families, and the community outreach agriculture functions throughout the year," states Charlotte Donn of the Vizcaya organization. Concluded in 1916, the Italian palazzo cost Deering $15 million. The celebration gathering began. "Vizcaya opened its doors on Christmas of 1916 with a pageant arranged by Paul Chalfin. As Deering stepped off his yacht onto the terrace, the lights of his villa came on in sequence, a line of thirty servants emerged from the loggia, and two cannons fired a salute. The evening's festivities were topped off by a masquerade ball," Historic Record states.

Can you imagine gazing at Biscayne Bay daily, and observing Architect Suarez completing his finishing work on the garden? Observers compared Vizcaya to the largest house in the United States, The Biltmore in Ashville, North Carolina. Deering enjoyed his palace home for 9 years during the winter season. The palace home had many modern conveniences, such as central vacuum systems, elevators and an indoor/outdoor pool. Air conditioning was installed in 1986.

James Deering died in September 1925 on a French steamship, returning to the United States. After his death, Vizcaya was inherited by his brother's children, two nieces, Marion C. Deering McCormick and Ely Deering M. Danielson. They contacted Paul Chalfin to open the estate as a museum in 1934. The nieces became frightened of the hurricanes; 1926, 1928, 1935, which overwhelmed the heirs and increased their maintenances costs. Hurricane of 1935 devastated the estate's gardens. In the 1940's they sold off large amounts of the acreage to build Miami's Mercy Hospital, through the Catholic Diocese of St. Augustine, Florida. Hurricane Andrew in August 1992, caused catastrophic loss to the gardens and flooded the villa's basement.

The Barge

The heirs negotiated an agreement with Miami-Dade County to purchase Vizcaya as an art museum. "In 1952 and 1955, the heirs conveyed the Main House, Village, and grounds to Dade County for $1.4 million, also donating all the collections and furnishings as part of the transaction". County Commissioners created in 1998 "the Vizcaya Museum and Trust as the governing body for Vizcaya," *Visions of Vizcaya* stated. Restoration and preservation continues today.

Everyone must visit the magnificent Vizcaya. Contact information is (305) 250-9133.

WHITEHALL (HENRY M FLAGLER'S HOUSE)

Palm Beach, Florida
Palm Beach County
National Landmark 2000

The Whitehall vista is one of exclusivity. The winter home of Henry Morrison Flagler in Palm Beach is a National Historic Landmark. Whitehall is nationally significant for its association with Flagler, one of the leaders of industry and commerce during the late 19th and early 20th Centuries. At the national level, the house's architectural significance is an exceptional Neoclassical Revival, a monumental marble palace of the Gilded Age, sometimes called "The Taj Mahal of North America."

Flagler placed his confidence in two young New York architects, John Carrere and Thomas Hastings, asking them "to build me the finest home you can think of." Other instructions by Flagler were to build a central, open Spanish style courtyard with a fountain. The two-story (three-story in front) building, topped by red Spanish-tiled roof, constructed of brick, covered with stucco and painted white. The building was set around the central court yard.

The exclusive house dazzles and overpowers, with six thick white Roman Doric columns, matched by five bays in the entrance portico, located near the double front bronze doors.

The 55-room house interiors was designed and furnished by Pottier and Stymus of New York. Carrere and Hastings designed the grand, 4,400 square feet (110 x 40) Marble Hall (entrance hall), with seven types of marble from Italy and Vermont. The massive marble hall is set off by a grand, dual-curved staircase leading to the second floor hall. One must see to believe the impressive rococo dome ceiling. The great hall furnishings showcase marble statues and benches.

A wrought iron fence surrounds the six-acre site enhancing the orange and palm tree in the garden setting. The site was adjacent to his first hotel, Royal Poinciana. Flagler selected this site carefully to observe his Breakers Hotel, as he was apprehensive of another fire.

Whitehall was Flagler's wedding gift to his third wife, Mary Lily Kenan. Her wedding request was a marble palace; she named the house, Whitehall, with pleasing aesthetics of an elaborate showplace. The exclusive house with furnishing cost roughly $4 million in 1902.

Whitehall quickly became the center of Palm Beach social activity. The entertainment queen, and accomplished hostess, Mary Lily was the central figure. The unavailable Flagler worked in his study on the construction of his massive overseas railroad project to Key West, his last accomplishment. After the grand finale of the railroad's completion in 1912, Flagler slipped on Whitehall's marble steps, and fractured his hip. He passed in 1913.

Following Flagler's death, Mary Lily returned to Whitehall for "high season" winter visits. She married again in 1916 to an "old beau," Robert Bingham of Louisville, Kentucky. Mary Lily died a year later. Her cause of death is suspect! Whitehall was willed to Mary Lily's niece, Louise Wise Lewis who sold Whitehall to a group of investors. They added an inharmonious ten-story tower in the rear of the house, and then called it an exclusive club. The investors intended to alter the great marble hall; however Flagler's granddaughter, Jean Flagler Matthews, purchased Whitehall, and razed the non-conforming tower, converting Whitehall to today's impressive museum.

The popular Flagler Museum opened to the public in February 1960. Visitors, mostly from outside of Florida, have grown to 100,000 annually. On your inclusive tour of the entertaining rooms, do not miss the opulent music room containing the largest pipe organ found in a private home; there a private organist performed for the Flagler's. The library is styled in Italian Renaissance with a prominent painting of H. Flagler over the fireplace.

The vast lavish white and gold ballroom glistens with jeweled chandeliers. Down the hall is the billiards room where H. Flagler entertained his male friends. The structure's southwest corner is Flagler's functional office, which no longer serves as The Palm Beach Historical Society office.

From the Marble Hall, located on the right is the famous French Salon, where Mary Lily received her guests. To the west, the formal dining room is finished in satinwood with green tapestry walls, with crystal and bronze chandeliers marking the four corners of the room, adding to the ambiance.

You can tour the upstairs bedroom suites and view the silk fabrics in the intimate morning rooms. The Flagler's bedroom contained their dressing rooms and private bathroom with a sunken bathtub. Whitehall's 16 guest rooms with private baths were often occupied by the family favorites and closest friends.

You can exit to the peaceful courtyard; the tranquil space that was one of Flagler's favorite spots.

On the southwest lawn, there is a striking, $5 million building, the Flagler Pavilion, which exhibits Flagler's restored private railroad car, the Rambler. Visitors can enjoy the amenities, dine in Café Des Beaux-Arts, and take in the breath-taking views of the waterway, and West Palm Beach, the city that Henry Flagler established.

On your next Landmark site visit, you can stroll down Worth Avenue, walk through the Via Mizner Arcade and plan your shopping trip. After your long walk, you need to check in at the Breakers Hotel for a good night.

WINDOVER ARCHEOLOGICAL SITE

Titusville, Florida
Brevard County

National Landmark 1987

All readers need to recognize the Windover Site is a burial area, discovered by accident that inadvertently provided abundant new DNA data for all archaeologist the world over, not just in Florida. The Windover Site provides extraordinary data of artifacts, burial practices, brain tissue, health, fabric arts, observations, skeletal material, violence and more astonishing research data. Significance of the Windover Site is prominent archaeological antiquity material dating back to the early Archaic period and defined to be from around 8000 to 1000 BC of North American pre-Columbian cultural development.

In 1984 a road construction, a backhoe operator, Steve Vanderjagt, working on a shallow bog pond, unearthed rock looking pieces. Steve knew Titusville had few rocks, so he descended from his backhoe cabin to check and discovered these rock pieces were skulls. The pond's remaining earth was left undisturbed for investigation. He contacted, his developers, EKS Corporation, and all work stopped. Investigation, excavations and bone radiocarbon analysis commenced. The bone analysis yielded dates, "7210 years and 7320 years." The developers "donated $60,000 worth of pumping equipment to drain the .25 acre pond for excavation." Department of

Anthropology, Florida State University received a million dollar grant to study the Windover Site.

The watery cemetery yielded 168 skeletons, "50% adults and 50% children, indicating a high mortality rate for children, as would be expected." Children were buried with their toys, wooden pestle-shaped object and the carapace of a small turtle. Adult skeleton ages ranged, both male and female, "to about 60 years," with adult male height 5 feet 9 inches (175cm)." Most were buried in a Flexed fetal position, "on their left side and with their heads turned to the west. The bodies were buried in clusters of five or six, with graves held down by sharpened stakes. The remains were wrapped in fabric for burial. "Thirty-seven of the graves contained woven fabrics," that yielded eighty-six pieces of fabric of different textile weaves. Excited Archaeologists stated, the complex woven cloth was made of plant fiber, probably palm. Windover fabrics are the most complex and diverse type of textile materials from this time period currently in the New World. These features suggest a population well adapted to an ecological area with substantial amounts of time, energy, and resources devoted to nonessential activated. These time activities patterns indicate a refined technology, beyond mere survival. Project Director, Glen Doran, clarified burial cloth is the oldest fabric recovered in this hemisphere.

The extraordinary discovery of "a lump of slippery, dark brown material inside a skull" indeed, the material was human brain tissue. How could brain tissue be preserved from black peat from thousands of years ago? Ninety-one skulls were found to contain brain tissue. The brains "were shrunken to a third their normal size, nevertheless, "brain hemispheres and convolutions were clearly intact." The researchers sent the intact skulls for X-rays, Cat Scans and MRI which showed recognizable brain structures. Under no circumstances have scientists had an opportunity to study ancient DNA. "The DNA indicated Asian origin and a rare haplotgroup, X, *Life and Death at Windover,* Dr. Rachel Wentz. Haplotype is a group of genes—that are inherited together from a single parent. Carbon dating of the Indian brain tissue determined the Indian village existed 6,990 to 8,150 years ago, plus or minus 150 years, placing the remains in the Archaic Period.

Favorable conditions occurred at the pond for burial practices. Probably, burials existed within 24 to 48 hours after death that preserved brain and bone tissue. In other words, tissue had less time to decompose. With peat covering the bodies, an anaerobic atmosphere was created, shutting out oxygen, bacteria, fungi that caused decomposition. The pond's water "breathed"---or could breathe for the buried. "Animals were less likely to disturb graves under peat and water."

Additional data gathered from Windover. The native Indians suffered from arthritis which still torments us today. Bones displayed rough joints and deformities. Jaws lines and teeth showed few cavities but gum abscesses were visible. Data indicates the present of violence. Five skulls, both adult and children, indicated depression type fractures resulting from a hard blow to the head. Other bones injuries observed were deflecting fractures on the lower left arm and around right eye orb.

Windover site gained world significance and attention by creating new hypothesis. After three field seasons of excavations, the pond's remaining earth was left undisturbed for future investigation.

The goal is to begin research in fifteen or twenty years, --- when new analytical techniques and approaches could justify the resumption. On February 2011, when the site closed, backhoe operator, Steve Vanderjagt returned and covered the pond to await for future investigation.

Ybor Street Car

YBOR CITY HISTORIC DISTRICT

Tampa, Florida
Hillsborough County

National Landmark 1990

Visionary Vicente Martinez-Ybor relocated his 1886 Cuban Cigar Development project near Tampa. The melting pot of ethnic groups lived and worked harmoniously in Ybor City. They built flourishing social clubs that provided medical care for the membership. These citizens strived to live their best possible lives.

The impressive leader, Vicente Martinez-Ybor transferred his cigar manufacturing business out of isolated Key West because of distribution problems. Ybor friends encouraged their leader to contemplate Tampa as a site by reason of its excellent port facilities and a newly completed railroad line. In 1885 Ybor purchased forty acres of land northeast of Tampa. He sold a portion of land to his friend, Ignacio Haya. Both men embarked on building factories. In this time frame 200 cigar factories were established. Today, only one, J.C. Newman Cigar Company, 2701 N. 16th Street, is in operation.

In April 1886, a large Key West fire destroyed Ybor's factory, so he concentrated his time and energy on the Tampa operations. V.M. Ybor business colleague, Eduardo Manrara encouraged him to purchase more land, due to the low price of scrubland. Together, they hired Gavino Gutierrez, to lay out a company town, utilizing the grid pattern that became known as Ybor City. Ybor's Land and Improvement Company originated to construct worker "housing and buildings and sell factory sites to other cigar manufactures," as stated in the Historic

Record. Many workers' housing, "La Casita", little houses, were of the "Shotgun" style and Ybor Vernacular styles. In latter part of 1886, "Ybor alone had constructed 176 worker houses and purchased the control of the streetcar line that connected Ybor City with Tampa, "states the Historic Record.

Italians arrived next, culturally mixing well with the Cubans and Spaniards. Italians engaged in small business and farming operations. The German immigrants were very significant to the cigar industry. "German cigar box art was considered the best of its kind in the world," L. Glenn Westfall, Research Study for the

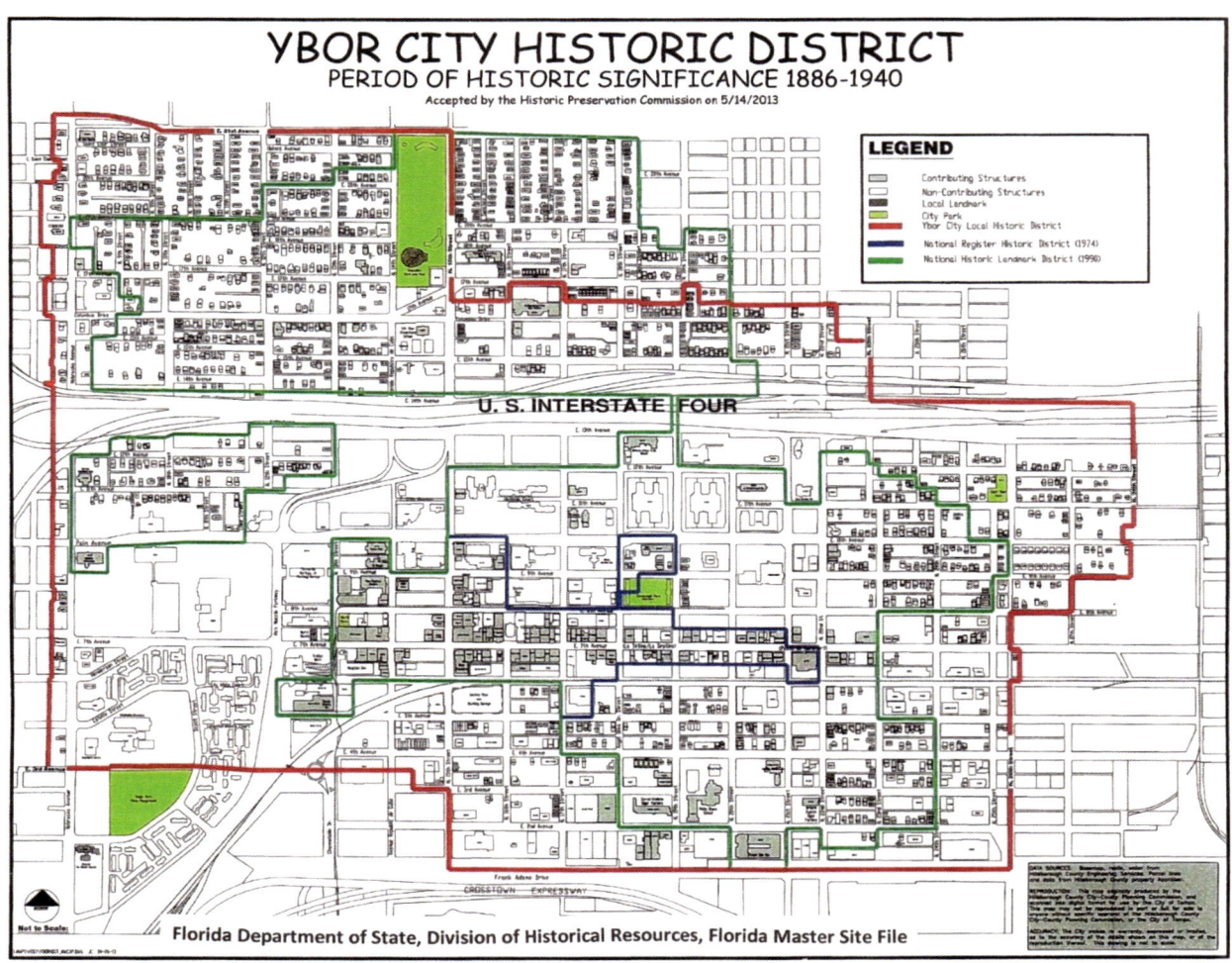

Rapid growth continued; by 1890 population estimates were fifteen thousand, mostly Cubans who moved from Key West and Cuba. Cubans were the hand rolled cigar makers and the hot, humid climate kept the tobacco workable. The next large ethnic group, Spaniards, arrived in 1900 for a sum total, of about 7,000. The

Development of Ybor City State Museum. "The Jews and Chinese …concentrated in the mercantile and service trades," Historic Record stated.

Cherokee Club, as originally known, became the El Pasaje Hotel. Cherokee Club was built by V.M. Ybor in 1895, as a businessman's club to exchange ideas and dealings. Tampa only had one hotel, Henry Plant's Tampa Bay Hotel, so Ybor transferred the building to an upscale hotel. During the Spanish-American War Army officers lodged there. Politician William Jennings Bryan was a guest. The building style is Italian Renaissance, two stories, brick, with a first-floor open arcade. Later M.V. Ybor utilized the site as his office and planned the construction of Ybor City and ran his businesses.

Vicente Martinez Ybor died on December 14, 1896, in Tampa, Florida. Most Tampa businesses closed to attend his funeral. His entombment is at Oaklawn Cemetery. A statue honors him in Ybor City, at Tampa's Riverwalk and at Centro Ybor shopping complex.

Multi-ethnic population is legendary for their social clubs. Ybor City's first and oldest club was El Centro Espanol De Tampa, founded by Spanish immigrants in 1891. The club is a National Landmark and has its individual chapter in this book. The complex club workings allowed a 5% extraction from worker pay checks for social membership fees and medical care. The clubs cared, socially and physically, for the entire workers families, welfare.

The Italians were next to start a social-medical club, known locally as the Italian Club, L'Unione Italiana, which became the cultural center for all Tampa. Fire destroyed the structure in 1914. The current neoclassical structure, three-and-one-half-stories, with four huge Roman Doric columns marks the main entrance, at the corner of Seventh Avenue and 18th Street.

The Cubans were focused on Cuban independence from Spain, thus they were the last committed to organizing a social club in 1902. They named the club El Circulo Cubano because the founders sat in group circle. The structure featured a unique amenity, a 900 seat theatre. Fire destroyed the first building. The group erected a new building, three-story, yellow brick, Beaux Arts Classic style on the same site, near the El Pasaje Hotel. The well, maintained building is still occupied.

The Germans formed a club at Nebraska and 11th Avenue. During World War I anti-German feelings developed. They sold the property to a Hebrew Association. City of Tampa now uses the building. The cultural tone was set among these ethnic working groups, as a unique city. English language was the second one spoken. Shop keepers posted signs, "English Spoken Here." Cigar manufacturing prospered from 1900 to 1929 with 200 working sites. "Success of the Tampa cigar was largely due to the skilled Latin craftsmen … who handcrafted cigars in 36 sizes and shapes" Historic Record states. Demand for good cigars did not continue because of a public increase of cigarette consumption. Improved machinery produced cigars comparable to hand-rolled ones. "The Depression hit the community hard, because cigars were a luxury item, many cigar workers lost their jobs and stopped paying their club dues,"

Historic Record states. Families relocated out of Ybor City to find new employment. Veterans returning from World War II failed to find employment in Ybor City. The downward spiral continued for Ybor City. Visible blight took on the appearance of an urban slum during the early 1960's. In 1965

Federal Urban Renewal Program demolished older residential and commercial structures with expectations of revitalizing the area. Additionally, Interstate 4 construction cut north-south routes through Ybor City, but this advantage gave an easy exit from I-4 to the city. Federal funds for redevelopment disappeared with budget cuts in 1980's.

These events stimulated interest, a new awareness among the Latin community to preserve its culture and significant buildings, and their "way of life in the neighborhood." A cultural anchoring neighborhood structure, greater than 100 years old, is the 1905 Columbia Restaurant that is representative of Ybor City. In 2019, it seats 1,700 customers in fifteen dining rooms. Columbia Restaurant has competition from 27 other restaurants in Ybor City today. Likewise, the cherished cultural heritage are the social clubs for the ethnic population. The goal became to retain and to improve the neighborhood that has architectural character and quality.

The records state, blossoming artists, seeking a good roof over their heads, searched for inexpensive studio units. In all likelihood, artist's actions fueled the cities "back to life" and started the Ybor City gentrification process, beginning about 1980s and continuing to the present day. "Gentrification is a process of renovating deteriorated urban neighborhoods by means of the influx of more affluent residents", Urban Planning definition. Services were needed, both retail and professional. Transportation, Ybor's yellow buses are always available. Entertainment and night clubs grew and expanded, reflecting the historic district's ranking as a party destination. Traffic and parking became an issue. The city built parking garages near 7th avenue for the visitors.

The Historic Preservation parameters set by the City of Tampa, Economic and Urban Development Department and Ybor City's Chamber of Commerce for the historic district prioritizes the redevelopment and restoration of its structures, and to improve the neighborhood, that reflects the cherished cultural heritage with architectural character. Landmark El Centro Espanol De Tampa had an adaptive reuse and combines with Centro Ybor. The two structures form a shopping complex/entertainment center. Hillsborough Community College maintains a campus in Ybor that offers a diverse program. Cigar factories are being renovated for residential uses. Completed large new apartments, Bainbridge and condominium complexes offer excellent housing choices, while other complexes are under construction. Hotel accommodations Hampton Inn, Hilton Garden Inn, and Ybor House-- can house most regional conferences, while more boutique hotels are under construction. The foodies can choose from 27 (estimate) restaurants for most cuisines. An interesting tour is the Official Ybor City Ghost Tour! Your Spiritual needs can be carefully chosen with 5 establishments of your choice. Real Estate and Financial services assists the forward motion.

Ybor City, is roughly a 26-block area, but this is unconfirmed in the data. Ybor City Development Corporation/ Economic and Urban Development Department (YCDC) supplied the 2016 Resident Population as

J. C. Newman Cigar Company

3,108. Population growth for 2018 is expected to increase by at least 240, the Bainbridge Apartment residents. In 2020 a new population census will complete the data. YCDC study addressed demographics, district priorities, expectation gaps, parking, transportation and summary notes. This excellent study is available to you by calling YCDC, (813) 274-7917, City of Tampa.

How beautifully everything is arranged, illustrating modern Ybor City's architectural character and the cherished cultural heritage. You can take a walking tour to witness the resilience, district uniqueness, and the protection of the historic buildings. Ybor City Ambassadors provide friendly guides and assist visitors.

Email your inquiry to: YborAmbassadors@tampagov.net or contact Ybor City Development Corporation at (813) 274-7936.

SELECTED READING AND RESOURCES

Akin, Edward. *Flagler: Rockefeller Partner and Florida Baron.* Gainesville: University Press of Florida, 1991

Boone, Floyd E. *Florida Historical Markers and Sites.* Houston, T Gulf Publishing Company,

Braden, Susan. *The Architecture of Leisure.* Gainesville: University Press of Florida2002
Caemmerer, Alex. *The Houses of Key West.* Sarasota: Pineapple Press, 1992

Catanese, Anthony and James Snyder. *Urban Planning.* New York: McGraw-Hill Book Company, 1989

Ching, Francis D. K. *A Visual Dictionary of Architecture.* New York: John Wiley & Sons, 1995

Clark, James C., *Hidden History of Florida.* Charleston: History Press, 2015.

De Quesada, A.M. *History of Florida's Forts.* Charleston: The History Press, 2013

Douglas, Stoneman Marjory. *Voice of the River. (Autobiography by Marjory S. Douglas with John Rothchild).* Sarasota: Pineapple Press, 1987

Elder, Amy A. *Portal to Florida's Past.* Sarasota: Peppertree Press, 2013

Holland, Keith, Lee B. Manley, Towart, James. *The Maple Leaf.* Jacksonville: St Johns Archaeological Expeditions, 1993.

Fairbanks, George R. *History and Antiquities of the City of St. Augustine, Florida.* Gainesville: University Press of Florida, 1975. Reprint.

Florida Department of State, Division Historical Resources, Bureau of Historic Preservation. Florida Master Site File, All 67 Counties. Tallahassee, Florida.

Florida Division of Recreation and Parks. 3900 Commonwealth Boulevard, Tallahassee, Florida 32399.

George, Paul, S. *A Guide to the History of Florida.* New York: Greenwood Press, 1989

Gleason, David King. *Over Miami.* Baton Rouge: Louisiana State University Press 1990.

Jahoda, Gloria. *The Other Florida.* Stuart: Southeastern Printing Company, 1967, 1984

Keys, Leslee, F. *Hotel Ponce De Leon.* Gainesville: University Press of Florida, 2015.

Kleinberg, Eliott. *Historical Traveler's Guide to Florida.* Sarasota: Pineapple Press, 1997.

LaHurd, Jeff. *Quintessential Sarasota.* Sarasota: Clubhouse Publishing, Inc. 1990

Martin, Sidney W. *Henry Flagler, Visionary of the Gilded Age.* Lake Buena Vista: Tailored Tours Publications, 1998.

McIver, Stuart B. *Hemingway's Key West.* Sarasota: Pineapple Press, 1993.

Murtagh, William J. *Keeping Time: The History and Theory of Preservation in America.* New York: John Wiley and Sons, Inc. 2005.

Nolan, David. *The Houses of St. Augustine.* Sarasota: Pineapple Press, 1998

Tim Ohr, Michael Sanders, James Phillips, Nevin Sitlin. *Florida's Historic Places.* Tampa: Rocky Publications, 2012

Plath, James and Frank Simons. *Remembering Ernest Hemingway.* Key West: Ketch & Yawl Press 1999.

Reeves, F. Blair. *A Guide to Florida's Historic Architecture.* Gainesville: University Press of Florida, 1989.

Tebeau, Charlton. *A History of Florida.* Coral Gables: University of Miami Press, 1972.

Waitley, Douglas. *Florida History from the Highways.* Sarasota: Pineapple Press, Inc. 2005.

Winsberg, Morton. *Florida's History Through Its Places.*

United States Department of the Interior, National Park Service, National Historic Landmarks Program, All (67) Counties. Washington, D.C.

Visions of Vizcaya, Miami: Vizcaya Museum and Gardens, 2006

Young, June Hurley. *Don Ce Sar Story*. St. Petersburg: Partnership Press, 1974